MANAGING STRESS WITH THE WORD OF GOD

MIRIAM KINAI

Copyright © 2006 Miriam Kinai

All rights reserved.

ISBN:996671510X
ISBN-13:978-9966715104

Scripture taken from the New King James Version.
Copyright © 1979, 1980, 1982 by Thomas Nelson, Inc.
Used by permission.
All rights reserved.

DEDICATION

This book is dedicated to the Lord God Almighty who protected, guided, strengthened and supported me through my stormy stressful situation.

**Blessed be the God and Father of our Lord Jesus Christ,
the Father of mercies and God of all comfort,
who comforts us in all our tribulation,
that we may be able to comfort
those who are in any trouble,
with the comfort with
which we ourselves
are comforted
by God.**
(2 Corinthians 1:3-4)

CONTENTS

	Acknowledgments	i
1	What is Stress?	Pg 9
2	What are the Symptoms of Stress?	Pg 11
3	Seek the Lord	Pg 17
4	Let Jesus In	Pg 27
5	Trust in the Lord	Pg 33
6	Transform Yourself	Pg 45
7	Position Yourself	Pg 55
8	Wait on the Lord	Pg 69
9	Medical Relaxation Techniques	Pg 83
10	Obey the Lord	Pg 105

ACKNOWLEDGMENTS

I would like to thank all the people who contributed to the experiences that culminated in writing of this book.

MIRIAM KINAI

❧1❦
WHAT IS STRESS?
(Define Stress)

Stress is the body's physiological response to any stimuli that requires a change in its physical, mental or emotional functioning.

There are many sources of stress. These include personal issues like illnesses, disabilities, unemployment, financial disasters, relationship problems, negative thoughts, worries, traumatic physical or sexual assaults or any other situation that disrupts or changes a person's life. Positive events such as getting a baby or a new job can also be a source of stress.

The source of stress can also be something devastating that has happened to someone dear to you such as their death, illness or addiction.

Stress in itself is not bad when it is under your control. Moderate doses of short term stress can help you think more creatively and perform more efficiently. It is when it gets out of your control that it begins to adversely affect your health, relationships and work performance.

THE BODY'S RESPONSE TO STRESS

Whatever the source of the stress, whether it is physical or mental, personal or social, real or imaginary, the human body responds in a uniform manner knows as the General Adaptation Syndrome which consists of 3 stages.

The first stage is the alarm reaction in which the nervous system is activated resulting in the release of the stress hormones adrenaline and noradrenaline from the adrenals.

The heart then begins to beat faster and the blood pressure rises in order to increase the blood supply to the brain, arm and leg muscles. This also enables swift decision making and their rapid execution.

The respiration rate also rises to increase the oxygen supply to these organs. Body stores of glucose and fats are released into the blood stream to provide energy. Perspiration also increases to cool the body in this state of emergency as it prepares to fight the stressor or flee from the stressful situation.

The second stage is the resistance stage in which the adrenal glands continue producing stress hormones to enable the body to continue fighting or resisting the stressor long after the effects of the fight or flight response have worn off.

The third stage is the exhaustion stage. This occurs when the stressful situation is prolonged or if one stressful event is quickly followed by another before the body is fully able to relax and recover from the first one.

The resultant prolonged bombardment of the various body organs by the circulating stress hormones results in physical and mental exhaustion and dis-ease or stress related illnesses in the body.

❧2❧

WHAT ARE THE

SYMPTOMS OF STRESS?

(How Do I Know I Am Stressed?)

Physical symptoms of stress include muscle aches, chest pains, palpitations, shortness of breath, constipation, diarrhea, appetite changes, weight gain or weight loss, tics and tremors, physical exhaustion and sleeping difficulties such us inability to fall asleep or waking up tired.

Mental symptoms of stress include poor concentration, difficulties making simple decisions, forgetfulness and mental exhaustion.

Emotional symptoms of stress include feeling moody, tearful, anxious, and depressed or that you cannot cope.

Behavioral symptoms are usually noticed by your family, friends and workmates who may complain your behavior has changed as you have become irritable, impatient, and very aggressive and have frequent angry outbursts. They may also report that you neglect your personal hygiene or appearance and have withdrawn socially.

In addition to this, chronic or longstanding stress causes or worsens many stress related diseases such as hypertension, diabetes, coronary heart disease, irritable bowel syndrome, peptic ulcers, migraine headaches, neck pains and backaches.

It also contributes to panic attacks, anxiety, depression, chronic fatigue syndrome, eczema exacerbations, menstrual period irregularities, decreased libido and suppresses the immune system.

WHY USE BIBLICAL PRINCIPLES WITH MEDICAL TECHNIQUES?

As stressful situations are inevitable in life, one needs an effective method to manage stress in order to avoid developing the numerous physical, mental, emotional and behavioral symptoms of stress. For a stress management method to be effective, it must address and resolve the root cause of the stress and not just medicate the symptoms of the stress.

Medically proven techniques such as those discussed in this book which include abdominal breathing, Christian meditation, Christian visualization and physical exercise are very effective in helping you cope with a stressful situation but they may not be able to address the root cause of the stress.

Combining medical techniques with problem solving strategies may also not address the root cause of the stress in some stressful situations. Examples of such situations include the death of someone you love dearly such as a spouse or a child, being afflicted with an incurable illness or it may be having to live with the physical and mental consequences of something terrible that was done to you.

In these and other similar situations where the root cause of the stress cannot be tackled by anything that this earth has to offer, one needs help from above to effectively deal with the stressful situation and this help can only be obtained from the Bible.

This is because **The Word of God is living and powerful ☐ piercing even to the division of soul and spirit** (Hebrews 4:12) where it can bring back to life those parts that died when you buried your loved ones. It can heal wounds and memories in places where bandages and even intravenous medications cannot reach and make you whole.

It is also able to sustain you in each and every situation that you may encounter in this life for **Man shall not live by bread alone; but man lives by every word that proceeds from the mouth of the Lord.** (Deuteronomy 8:3)

Therefore, the Biblical principles discussed in this book which include Seek the Lord or Prayer, Let Jesus in or Salvation, Trust in the Lord or Faith, Transform yourself or Scriptural mental transformation, Position yourself or Work, Wait on the Lord or Patience and Obey God or Obedience are drawn from the Word of God so that they can sustain you even in those stressful situations without an earthly solution.

Therefore, by combing Biblical principles with medical techniques, you will be able to manage any stressful situation that you may encounter in this life.

This combination will also enable you to rapidly break the vicious cycle in which stress results in stress related illnesses which in turn increase the stress in your already stressful situation.

Managing Stress with the Word of God will therefore guide you through this very effective holistic approach to managing stress. It begins with the spiritual aspect (Chapter 3 to 5), then it moves on to the mental aspect (Step 6) and finally to the physical aspect (Step 7 to 10).

May you be blessed as you read this book and in turn help someone with the wisdom that you will gain from your stressful situation.

Dr. Miriam Kinai.

MANAGING STRESS WITH THE WORD OF GOD

The Storm Strikes

You are in your boat.
You are paddling down the sea of life minding your own business. All is fine as the sun is smiling, the sea serene, and the view splendid. You know your destination, your compass is set and your supplies are sufficient.

Suddenly, you are drowning.
The murky waters are filling your mouth and you are struggling to remain afloat. You are not sure what happened. All you can remember is a lightning flash of pain searing through your mind and flesh.

Everything has changed.
The sun, skies and sea have turned gray and you can no longer tell whether it is day or night. The blackness of the darkness is closing in on you as the waves pull you down. They are all against you.

Everything you had is lost.
You have lost your mobile, map, compass and supplies. Your boat is upside down and the wind is pulling it away from you. You have also lost your self-sufficiency, sense of direction and peace of mind.

You scramble into your boat.
You begin paddling furiously to get back to the shore even though you don't know where that is anymore. You can't tell whether you are advancing or regressing but you paddle anyway.

Predators position themselves.
Birds of prey are swooping in the sky surveying their next meal. Sharks encircle you scrutinizing their next snack. The pounce simultaneously and your right eye is pecked out as your left arm is clipped out.

You are bleeding profusely.
The sea casually buries your precious lifeblood in its waves. The birds rejoice and call their pals to celebrate. The sharks feast and plan the next attack. No one cares about you.

Hope ebbs away.
Fear rises, optimism falls, worries surge and faith fails as your emotions rise and fall with the waves. Clouds of gloom gather and rain discouragement to drown you in despair.

You break down.
The stress is too much. You can't bear it anymore. You can't row any further. You are emotionally and physically exhausted. You ache all over as your heart is now pumping pain.

You break it down.
You realize can't fight on two fronts and win. You have to calm your inner storm first if you are going to survive the outer one. You look up to the sky and cry out "Jesus, son of David have mercy on me".

You submit to Jesus.
You let Him into your heart and let Him Captain your life boat through the stormy stressful situation. His peace calms your inner storm as fear flows away, worries wash away and despair lifts.

You discern His presence.
In your stillness within the eye of the storm you come to understand that He is still God and still in control even if the wind and waves seem to be out of control.

He is talking to you.
He is speaking silently but you can hear Him loud and clear amid the howling wind. He tells you how to position yourself and where to row your boat.

The outer storm can't stress you now.
The wind and waves may rock your boat, but you are anchored securely in the Rock of the Ages. The predators may hurt you, but He heals. It no longer matters what the night may bring your way for you know that you are held securely in the palm of His Hand.

1

SEEK THE LORD
(Pray)

It happened after this that the people of Moab with the people of Ammon, and others with them besides the Ammonites, came to battle against Jehoshaphat. Then some came and told Jehoshaphat, saying, "A great multitude is coming against you from beyond the sea, from Syria; and they are in Hazazon Tamar (which is En Gedi). And Jehoshaphat feared and set himself to seek the Lord, and proclaimed a fast throughout all Judah. So Judah gathered together to ask help from the Lord; and from all the cities of Judah they came to seek the Lord. (2 Chronicles 20:1-4)

The first thing that you should do when you are faced by any stressful situation is to seek the Lord and inquire from Him what you should do about it.

Pray and ask Him to fill you with the wisdom and understanding that His Spirit gives so that you may know the right thing to do regardless of whether your stressful situation is due to your health failing, your family fighting or your finances floundering.

Seek the Lord first and **Do not be wise in your own eyes.** (Proverbs 3:7) Do not rush to make any decision, speak hastily or hurry to do whatever you think may be the right thing to do at that particular time. Ask for the Lord's direction first like King Jehoshaphat. He did not first order his army to prepare for war even though one of their cities had already being captured by the attackers. He first sought the Lord to find out what they were to do about their stressful situation.

Cry out to Him even in an emergency for He says, **Call to Me, and I will answer you, and show you great and mighty things, which you do not know.** (Jeremiah 33:3) Therefore, pray and you may receive new insights or get a different outlook into your situation that will enable you make more constructive decisions.

SEEK GOD FIRST, NOT FRIENDS

Seek the Lord's direction first before you seek the recommendations of friends and specialists for people are not able to see the entire picture as God is able to see it from His Heavenly perspective.

When Job was faced with his stressful situation, his friends thought God was punishing him because of his sinfulness and their advice was based on this (mis)understanding yet nothing could have been further from the truth than this for in God's own words, Job was a man who feared Him, was blameless, upright and shunned evil. (Job 1:8)

The same could also be true for you. Your family and friends are looking at your stressful situation and interpreting it according to their insight and character. Their appraisal and resultant advice may or may not be accurate.

Therefore, seek God's advice first for He knows everything about your situation including the person who can best help you.

GO TO A SOLITARY PLACE

When you are dealing with a stressful situation, you need to regularly retreat to a solitary place where you can pray. Schedule a time and designate a place where you can go to be by yourself with God.

It can be just 10 min a day to begin with, but it is a sacred appointment that you must honor just as you would any other important meeting. It can be at any hour of the day but it must be at a time when you can be alone without interruptions. Mornings are the ideal time because you have not yet been encumbered by the stresses of the day.

Your solitary place should preferably be a private refuge where you can go to flee your stressors. It can be your bedroom, your office, a church or even a park that you pass by every day.

Once you are in your solitary place, write down all the things that are stressing you from the most distressing to the least distressing before you begin praying. This is because writing down your problems enables you to express your feelings and say in written words exactly what is on your mind and in your heart without hurting anyone. Keep writing until you have nothing more to get off your chest and you feel relieved for this release will leave you less emotional and more objective about your stressful situation as you begin to pray for it.

If you are not able to physically leave your stressful situation and go to a solitary place, then you can escape to your solitary space. You can create this space by mentally withdrawing from your surroundings. You can tune out the world and tune in to God in prayer as you walk to the bus stop or train station every morning or even as you are driving home from work. You can even withdraw during a stressful situation such an argument, when you can begin to pray in silence for His guidance.

PRAY WITH CONFIDENCE

After you escape to your solitary place or space to pray, you have to pray with the confidence that God is listening to you and He will answer your prayers.

You have to have faith in your prayers for in some stressful situations you may find that there is no one you can ask to pray for you. This may be because you have no one whom you can fully confide in about your situation or you may feel that you are protecting the people you love by not telling them your problems because you know that they already have enough problems of their own. Or you may be faced by a sudden, urgent crisis in which you have no time to call anyone to pray for you or you may even find that your stressful situation has isolated you and no one wants to be associated with you.

Whatever your circumstances, do not give up on yourself and on your stressful situation just because you are the only one praying for yourself.

The Bible assures us that **We do not have a High Priest who cannot sympathize with our weaknesses, but was in all points tempted as we are, yet without sin. Let us therefore come boldly to the throne of grace, that we may obtain mercy and find grace to help in time of need.** (Hebrews 4: 15-16)

Therefore, regardless of your past mistakes or your present life situation, you can still pray with confidence and God will listen because He is merciful. He is able to sympathize with you in your predicament and He will help you out in your hour of need.

He also promises us that **You will call upon Me and go and pray to Me, and I will listen to you. And you will seek Me and find Me, when you search for Me with all your heart.** (Jeremiah 29: 12-13)

Therefore stop whatever you are doing and earnestly seek the Lord with your entire being. Pray with confidence because He is listening to you, He will come to your aid and you can triumph over your stressful situation even if no one else is praying for you.

ACKNOWLEDGE THAT HE IS GOD

So Judah gathered together to ask help from the Lord; and from all the cities of Judah they came to seek the Lord. Then Jehoshaphat stood in the assembly of Judah and Jerusalem, in the house of the Lord, before the new court, and said: "O Lord God of our fathers, are You not God in heaven, and do You not rule over all the kingdoms of the nations, and in Your hand is there not power and might, so that no one is able to withstand You? Are You not our God, who drove out the inhabitants of this land before Your people Israel, and gave it to the descendants of Abraham your friend forever?" (2 Chronicles 20:4-7)

When you pray for your situation, begin by acknowledging that God is in control of all things in heaven and here on earth including your stressful situation. Confess that there is no problem that is too big for Him or that He cannot solve and that there is no situation so stressful that He cannot resolve for He is the Almighty God.

King Jehoshaphat acknowledged that God was the One who had given them the land that they were dwelling on and so they believed that He was also able to protect it from those who were invading it.

If you are suffering from a physical disease, declare that since God created your body, He is also able to heal it.

If there is a rift in your marriage, proclaim that since He is the one who joined you and your spouse, He is also able to keep you together for **What God has joined together, let not man separate.** (Matthew 19:6)

CAST YOUR BURDENS ON THE LORD

After acknowledging the Lord's sovereignty over your stressful situation, you should now **Humble yourselves under the mighty hand of God, that He may exalt you in due time, casting all your care upon Him, for He cares for you.** (1 Peter 5: 6-7)

He cares for you and you do not have to develop backaches from carrying burdens that are too heavy for you or develop headaches from trying to figure out how you are going to solve all your problems. All you have to do is to **Cast your burden on the Lord, and He shall sustain you.** (Psalm 55: 22)

Cast all the problems arising out of your stressful situation to the Lord in prayer. Cast all the people who are stressing you to Him so that He can deal with them. Cast your entire stormy stressful situation and all its attendant frustrations and uncertainties to Him and promise yourself that once you have released your burdens you will never pick them up again.

Let Him carry them for you since you cannot move forward if you are always agonizing over the same anxieties or aggravated by the same old problems. You have to lay them down once and for all and then ask Him for what you need.

ASK IN FAITH

After casting all your stressors to the Lord, you can now ask in faith for whatever you need to resolve your stressful situation for He tells us, **Ask, and it will be given to you** (Matthew 7:7)

To receive what you are asking for, you have to believe that you will receive it for His Word urges us to **Ask in faith, with no doubting, for he who doubts is like a wave of the sea driven and tossed by the wind. For let not that man suppose that he will receive anything from the Lord; he is a double-minded man, unstable in all his ways.** (James 1:6-8)

Since **Faith is the substance of things hoped for, the evidence of things not seen** (Hebrews 11:1), asking in faith entails being able to see yourself with your mind's eye receiving the things that you are asking the Lord to give you.

If you are asking for healing, you have to see the laboratory tests returning as normal, the cancerous mass becoming undetectable and the doctors telling you that you have been cured.

If you are praying for your family to be restored, you have to see your marital problems resolving and the wayward child coming back home.

If you are praying for a financial breakthrough, you have to see yourself receiving the appointment letter and cashing the checks.

See it, pray believing that the Lord can bring it to pass and then live expecting to receive it.

NEVERTHELESS

O My Father, if it is possible, let this cup pass from Me; nevertheless, not as I will, but as You will. (Matthew 26: 39)

This nevertheless is an important part of your prayers as it allows you to express your desires, wants and needs fully to God and then opens you up to be fully receptive to what He desires and wants from you.

The nevertheless is very important because your prayers should not be to impose your will on God, but rather to align yourself to Him and submit to His will for your life just as Jesus did.

You do not have to fear when you pray this type of open ended prayer for He says **I know the thoughts that I think toward you, says the Lord, thoughts of peace and not of evil, to give you a future and a hope.** (Jeremiah 29:11)

PRAY WITH THANKSGIVING

Finally, after you have cast your burdens, asked for what you need and submitted to God's will for your life and situation, you can now thank Him. Thank Him for the blessings that He has already bestowed on you and for the blessings that you are expecting to receive in faith.

ACTION PLAN

1. Schedule a time in your daily diary when you will escape to your solitary place or space to be alone with God to pray.

2. Write down all the things that are stressing you from the most distressing to the least distressing. Let this be your prayer list and pray over each item asking God to direct you and tell you what you should do about each one of them.

3. Buy a note book and label it **GOD IS FAITHFUL**. Everyday write down three blessings that you are grateful for. These may include your life, your health, your family, your job, preaching that ministered to your specific need or timely help you received from a stranger.

LET US PRAY

Hear my prayer, O Lord, and listen to my supplications. In your faithfulness answer me, for (name your stressful situation) *has oppressed me. It has crushed my life to the ground. I am in deep despair and my heart within me is distressed.*

Answer me speedily, O Lord for my spirit fails! Do not hide your face from me. Remind me each morning of your constant love for in You do I trust. Cause me to know the way in which I should walk for I lift up my soul to You.

Deliver me, O Lord, from (name your stressful situation) *for in You I take shelter. Teach me to do Your will, for You are my God. Guide me on a safe path*

Rescue me, O Lord, for your name's sake! For your righteousness sake bring my soul out of trouble. In your mercy save me from (name your stressful situation) *and destroy all that trouble my soul for I am Your servant.* (Adapted from Psalm 143)

❧4❧

LET JESUS IN
(Get Saved)

Behold, I stand at the door and knock. If anyone hears My voice and opens the door, I will come in to him and dine with him, and he with Me. (Revelation 3:20)

To successfully manage any stressful situation, you have to let Jesus into your heart and into your life so that He can calm your inner stormy emotions and show you how to manage your outer stormy stressful situation.

Jesus has taken the first step. He came to earth, was crucified for our sins and now He stands at the door of your heart knocking. He knocks and waits for you to let Him in voluntarily. He will not coerce you or force His way in. You have to admit to yourself that you need divine help and then make the conscious choice of letting Him into your life.

Even if your entire life is in a mess because you dabbled in the occult, abused drugs, flirted with immorality and broke all the commandments, Jesus still wants to come into your life and that is why He stands at your soiled door knocking.

He already knows what type of chaos you are living in so do not be afraid or ashamed of your mess **For God did not send His Son into the world to condemn the world, but that the world through Him might be saved. He who believes in Him is not condemned; but he who does not believe is condemned already.** (John 3:17-18)

So let Jesus in right now so that He can help you sort out your life and your stressful situation. You can let Him in today when you are stressed or you can let Him in tomorrow when you are even more stressed by your problems. The choice is yours. When do you want the change? If you want it now, open the door and **Do not harden your hearts as in the rebellion.** (Psalm 95:8)

Opening the door of your heart to Jesus or getting saved is very simple. All you have to do is to turn away from your sins and then **You confess with your mouth the Lord Jesus and believe in your heart that God has raised Him from the dead, you will be saved. For with the heart one believes unto righteousness, and with the mouth confession is made unto salvation.** (Romans 10:9-10)

Acknowledge that Jesus is Lord and then lay your entire life before Him so that the healing can begin. Let Him see what the stress has done to you. Show Him the cracks in the walls of your mind that keep extending everyday as your problems become more and more unbearable.

Show Him the windows of your heart patched up with old newspapers that will not let the light of love in after the panes were shattered by unfaithful loved ones.

Show Him the rooms in your head that you will not enter as they are haunted by broken dreams and wasted opportunities.

Let Him smell the stench from the garbage that you brought home one evening, grew attached to and have been unable to throw out.

Let Him see the taps that will not close, dripping tears of agony day after day, night after night. Show Him the toilets that will not flush and let go of painful memories as they are clogged with bitterness and hatred.

Unveil the wounds on your body that you have been hiding. Let Him see the hand that was amputated by the accident, the eye that was blinded by the assault, the mastectomy scar and the kidneys that have failed due to diabetes. Show Him the limitations imposed on you by your financial setbacks - the vital medications you cannot afford, the meals you forego and the clothes peeling off your back. Let Him see the full extent of your depravity so that He can restore you to wholeness.

Do not fear to bare it all for Him for He looks with love and listens with compassion. What you are unable to express in words, He is able to read from your heart. He can understand all those subtle nuances of anguish that you cannot verbalize.

He will also not flinch in disgust at the state you are in for He even wants to eat with you. He wants to share in your stress and suffering for He has accepted you. He loves you just as you are, right where you are. So let Him in and let Him be the Friend who will walk with you through it all for He is the only One who can see it all and solve it all.

SUBMIT TO GOD (James 4: 7)

After you have laid your entire life in front of Him, you now have to submit to Him. Let Jesus take control and be Lord over your heart, your mind and your body.

Surrender to Him unconditionally because He loves you with an unconditional love. Surrender your hurting heart, your broken life, your present stressful situation and your uncertain future. Surrender it all to Him and do not sequester any part of your life away from Him. Let Him have His way.

If you are used to having things done your way and your way only, yield to His will. Relinquish your plans and let Jesus show you what He has planned for you. Do not hold back because you fear that His agenda for your life may not be what you want for yourself.

God designed you for a specific purpose **For we are His workmanship, created in Christ Jesus for good works, which God prepared beforehand that we should walk in them.** (Ephesians 2:10). Let Him lead you to fulfill your purpose.

Let Him also direct how you should manage your stressful situation. He will show you what to clean out first, what to throw away next and what to do after that. Follow His leading and you will find rest even in the middle of your stressful situation.

YOU WILL FIND REST

Come to Me, all you who labor and are heavy laden, and I will give you rest. Take My yoke upon you and learn from Me, for I am gentle and lowly in heart, and you will find rest for your souls. For my yoke is easy and My burden is light. (Matthew 11:28-30)

If you are tired of struggling, learn from Jesus and live as He did. Take up His yoke or the instructions for living that He sets for us to follow and He will give you His peace.

Drop the heavy yoke of trying to live up to the world's a million and one ever changing expectations. Put on the simple one of living only to please God and you will find the peaceful rest that the world cannot give you.

Learn how He expects you to live by reading the Bible for **All Scripture is given by inspiration of God, and is profitable for doctrine, for reproof, for correction, for instruction in righteousness, that the man of God may be complete, thoroughly equipped for every good work.** (2 Timothy 3:16-17)

As you read the Word of God, pray for your eyes to be opened with understanding so that you may be able to discern its truths and its message. Think about the lessons that you can extract from each chapter to apply to your life.

Reading the Word is not enough, for you have to **Be doers of the word, and not hearers only, deceiving yourselves.** (James 1:22) Live as His word says you should and let it be the light that illuminates the path that you will walk on from this day forth.

ACTION PLAN

1. Confess with your mouth the Lord Jesus and believe in your heart that God has raised Him from the dead, you will be saved. (Romans 10:9)

2. Read at least one chapter of the Bible every day.

3. Each week begin doing one new thing that the Bible says you should do as you strengthen your walk with the Lord. You can begin with the first commandment (Deuteronomy 5:6-21) and work your way down to the tenth.

LET US PRAY

Have mercy upon me O God, because of your loving-kindness
Because of Your many tender mercies, wash away all my sins and cleanse me from my evil ways for I admit that I have sinned and my sins are always before me.

Wash me and I shall be whiter than snow.
Create in me a pure heart O God and renew a faithful and loyal spirit within me.

Do not remove me from Your presence and do not take away from me Your Holy Spirit.
Reestablish in me the joy of Your salvation and support me by your generous Spirit.
(Adapted from Psalm 51)

❧5❦

TRUST IN THE LORD
(Have Faith)

Blessed is the man who trusts in the Lord, and whose hope is the Lord. (Jeremiah 17:7)

After you have let Jesus into your life, if you want to be at peace all the time, you have to trust Him all the time.

Decide here and now that you are going to trust Him completely so that you are always on an even keel. Resolve to trust Him all the time so that you are not happy and hopeful one day and then hapless and hopeless the next.

Do not let past painful experiences make you transfer your mistrust of humans to God. Do not trust Him half-heartedly because of the heartache you experienced after you trusted people who turned out to be deceitful for **God is not a man, that He should lie.** (Numbers 23:19)

Even if you have never been let down by people know that **It is better to trust in the Lord than to put confidence in man** (Psalm 118:8) for no matter how bad or humiliating the situation may get, He will be with you and He will not bail out on you when you are hardest hit by problems.

Understand also, that no one else is more deserving of your unfaltering trust and utter dependence for not only does He promise you that He will never leave you nor forsake you (Hebrews 13:5) but He can also calm the wind or make you walk on the waves.

DO NOT WORRY

Then He said to His disciples, Therefore I say to you, do not worry about your life, what you will eat; nor about the body, what you will put on. Life is more than food, and the body is more than clothing. Consider the ravens, for they neither sow nor reap, which have neither storehouse nor barn; and God feeds them. Of how much more value are you than the birds? And which of you by worrying can add one cubit to his stature? (Luke 12:22-25)

Understand that you cannot correct any defective situation in your life by worrying about it. If you are stressed because your health is failing, worrying will not improve it. If you are stressed because your marriage is threatened, worrying will not protect it. If you are stressed because your finances are dwindling, worrying will not increase them. Regardless of your specific stressful situation, worrying will not help it because worry achieves nothing productive.

Worrying warps your thinking by winding a trail of what ifs around your mind. Mentally running through this maze wastes your time and energy because it takes you nowhere for your problems are still as they were (if not worse) than when you set out worrying and yet you are mentally exhausted.

Instead of wasting your time worrying, set aside some time when you are in your solitary place with God to find solutions for your worrisome challenges.

Write down your challenges in order of priority then ask God to help you as you brainstorm and write down all the possible solutions to each of them.

When you get a viable solution, decide when you will act on it and commit yourself to its execution.

If you do not get a solution at that point in time, leave the worrisome challenge with God and do not think about it during the day until the next time you are in your solitary place with Him. By doing this, you will not let worrisome thoughts run aimlessly around your mind when you are supposed to be working. Consciously refuse to dwell on them when they come into your mind because you know that you have a time and a place to deal with them.

For those worrisome challenges that you cannot think of any solution, forward them to the Lord and permanently delete them from your mind as they are now in His inbox and you have faith that He is able to manage them.

If you deal with all your challenges in this way you will never have anything to worry about because trusting God is the antidote to worrying. Therefore, **Be anxious for nothing, but in everything by prayer and supplication, with thanksgiving, let your requests be made known to God; and the peace of God, which surpasses all understanding, will guard your hearts and minds through Christ Jesus.** (Philippians 4: 6-7)

AT PEACE

As you get in the habit of trusting God with all your challenges, you will find that it is a very liberating step in managing stress for it sets your mind free from the oppression of worry and enables you to relax.

When your mind is not focused on your problems but it is focused on God whom you are trusting to help you solve them, you are able to relax because you will be at peace for His Word promises that **You will keep him in perfect peace, whose mind is stayed on You, because he trusts in You.** (Isaiah 26:3)

You will be able to be at peace even if the problems are still present in your life. You will be at peace whether the disease has left your body or not because you trust that God will take care of you either way. You will be at peace whether your finances have recovered or they are still ailing because you trust that He will take care of you regardless of your financial situation.

You will be at peace in the middle of your stressful situation and you will be able to testify that you are **Hard pressed on every side, yet not crushed; ☐ perplexed, but not in despair; persecuted, but not forsaken; struck down, but not destroyed** (2 Corinthians 4: 8-9) because you trust God completely.

You will be so peaceful that you will even be able to sleep in the middle of your storm because you trust the Master at the helm completely even if you don't understand why the storm is taking so long to calm down.

TRUST GOD BLINDLY

Some stressful situations are very perplexing. You cannot fathom how or why it is happening to you. You were rowing your boat minding your own business, the sun was shining, the sea calm, you knew where you were going, your compass was set, you had ample supplies and everything was just fine. Then, in the twinkling of an eye, you are in the middle of a raging storm, clutching to the edge of your capsizing boat.

You don't know what hit you. You didn't even see it coming. You can't understand why it would hit a nonviolent person like you so hard. Your boat was a specially designed model that was supposedly unable to capsize yet you are in the water. The meteorologist forecasted a warm sunny day with gentle winds yet the waves are titanic!

In your situation, you may be stressed right now because even though you had annual physical checkups, you ate healthily and exercised religiously, you have been diagnosed to have bilateral breast cancer at the age of 35!

Other stressful situations are inexplicable because a volcano of problems suddenly erupts in your life. You had no inkling that they were developing yet right now they are full blown and they have ripped your life apart.

In your situation, you may be stressed because you are the deacon in charge of youth counseling, you have brought up your children in the church, you have monitored them and kept the lines of communication open yet your 16 year old is pregnant and has HIV!

In other circumstances, you may be stressed not because the events have happened, but because you cannot explain how they have happened to you. You took all the precautions, played the game by all the rules and frankly speaking you are not the type of person that such things happen to. These are the type of things that you associated with other people's lives, other people's children, other people's careers but not your own.

In your situation, you may be stressed because you were the picture perfect husband/wife whom the married men/women at church admired and sought advice from. You honestly thought that your relationship with your spouse was perfect yet you are separating!

Whatever your actual stressful situation may be, when you suddenly find yourself in an incomprehensible stressful situation that you wish was a nightmare, yet it is your reality, do not try to understand why it is happening just yet.

Do not try to understand it right now because your perception of the predicament may be tinted red by anger or your judgment blunted by the shock. Understand that the more you just can't see the reason why it has happened, the more you should blindly trust in the Lord to show you your way through it all.

Entrust the whole situation to God, **Acknowledge Him, and He shall direct your paths.** (Proverbs 3:6) Let go of your need to understand the WHY and just say to Him, **Cause me to know the WAY in which I should walk, for I lift up my soul to You.** (Psalm 143:8)

Focus on finding out what God wants you to do at that particular time and then do it as you continue trusting Him. After you have done it, ask Him what you should do next then focus on doing it. In this way you will be able to move forward through your stressful situation even though you are blinded by pain and tears.

In other circumstances, you may have a rough idea of why the situation occurred, but you must still **Trust in the Lord with all your heart, and lean not on your own understanding.** (Proverbs 3:5). The more you just don't get it fully, the more you should fully trust His understanding and let Him guide you.

Even after the shock and anguish subside, you may never really fully comprehend why the stressful situation had to come into it your life and at that particular time because He tells us, **My thoughts are not your thoughts, nor are your ways My ways, says the Lord. For as the heavens are higher than the earth, so are My ways higher than your ways, and My thoughts than your thoughts.** (Isaiah 55: 8-9)

Recognize therefore, that the more your stressful situation does not make sense to you, the more you should stop trying to make sense out of it and trustfully rely on Him to work it out whether you are facing one gigantic challenge or multiple recurring challenges.

TRUSTING IN GIGANTIC CHALLENGES

If you are facing a very big challenge that has had devastating consequences on your life, you can learn from the story of Lazarus.

When Lazarus became sick, his sisters Martha and Mary sent a message to Jesus telling Him that he was sick. On getting the message, Jesus said, **This sickness is not unto death, but for the glory of God, that the Son of God may be glorified through it.** (John 11:4)

This was not something that Martha and Mary could have known as they watched their brother's condition worsen until he died. They could not have understood why Jesus delayed in coming to see his dear friend and came after Lazarus had already been dead and buried for four days.

They could not have foreseen that the people who had come to mourn and bury their brother would see him being raised from the dead and they would believe that Jesus really was the Son of God.

Though Martha, Mary and even Lazarus himself could not have known that his sickness and resultant death was for a larger purpose, Jesus knew.

Therefore, if you are going through some very difficult times as you bury people who are dear to you, or you are stressed because your precious marriage, ministry, business or career is dying and you don't understand why its dying, do not let these events stop you from trusting God.

Continue trusting in His wisdom for you cannot see the entire big picture and how this current loss of yours fits into His divine purposes.

Understand also that there may be people around you who are watching you manage your very challenging situation under the direction of the Lord Jesus and they will glorify God when they see Him heal what is ailing and revive what had died in your life.

They may be others who do not believe in God but when they witness the miraculous way in which your situation will unfold, they will believe and give glory to Him because of what they have seen in your life.

You may not even be aware that these people are watching you as you are so entombed in your grief but keep your faith and trust God especially when you do not understand why you are being afflicted in this particular way and at this particular time in your life.

Keep trusting Him for His Word tell us that **All things work together for good to those who love God, to those who are the called according to His purpose** (Romans 8:28) and this includes both positive and seemingly negative events in our lives.

TRUST GOD IN RECURRENT CHALLENGES

If you keep facing one stressful event after another, trust in God's Wisdom and learn from David's experiences.

David said to Saul, "Your servant used to keep his father's sheep, and when a lion or a bear came and took a lamb out of the flock, I went out after it and struck it, and delivered the lamb out from its mouth; and when it rose against me, I caught it by its beard, and struck and killed it. Your servant has killed both lion and bear; and this uncircumcised Philistine will be like one of them" The Lord, who delivered me from the paw of the lion and from the paw of the bear, He will deliver me from the hand of this Philistine. (1 Samuel 17: 34-37)

David's faith and confidence in God was strengthened by the recurring stressful situations that he faced as a shepherd when lions and bears would attack his flock and steal his lamb for he learned that he could depend on God to help him overcome any challenge regardless of how dangerous it was.

We can also see that through these recurring challenges, God had been preparing David out in the pastureland away from the "real" battlefield to fight the big battle with Goliath. This was the Goliath whom the other "real" soldiers who had been spending their time in the "real" battlefield were afraid of.

Therefore, since David had experienced God's protection first hand while fighting the lions and bears all alone, Goliath size and armor did not make him tremble. He knew with certainty that just as God had helped him kills lions and bears, He would also help him kill Goliath.

Likewise, if you are in a situation right now where life threatening problems keep attacking you one after another, trust in God even if you do not understand why your life has to unfold like that.

Trust that He is aware of all the tears that you have cried, all the battles that you have fought, all the losses you have incurred, the injustices that you are facing and all the dangers that are still encircling you. Trust that He is aware of your entire situation and He knows exactly what to do about it.

Understand also that God may have placed you in the shepherd position that you are in right now not so much to take care of sheep but mainly to learn how to deal with the lions and bears that are attacking you by learning to depend on Him. He may be using the challenges that you are facing right now to strengthen your faith and increase your spiritual warfare skills as He prepares you for the big task that He has in store for you in the future.

Therefore, keep trusting Him no matter how big the bears are that keep attacking you for He will not let more bears attack you than you can bear. (I Corinthians 10:13)

ACTION PLAN

1. If you have worrisome challenges deal with them in the following way when you are in your solitary space with God after asking for His guidance.
a. Write down all your worrisome challenges in order of priority.
b. Beginning with the most pressing worrisome challenge, think and write down all of its possible solutions
c. Set a commitment date when you will undertake each of the solutions to your worrisome challenge.

For example
a. Worrisome challenges in order of priority: Disease worsening, losing my job, being unable to pay the rent
b. Solutions for the disease worsening challenge: Consult a doctor, eat nutritiously, take a multivitamin, pray for myself, be prayed for by my Pastor
c. Commitment date for the disease worsening challenge:
Pray for myself – immediate
Eat healthy foods – from supper tonight
Take a multivitamin – from tomorrow morning
Prayers by my Pastor – request him on Sunday
Consult a doctor – book an appointment for Monday

As you do each of the activities in your action plan tick them off and then move on to brainstorm for solutions and set up an action plan for your next most pressing challenge.

1. Answer the following question:
Behold, I am the Lord, the God of all flesh. Is there anything too hard for me? (Jeremiah 32:27)

2. Meditate on the following scripture:
All things work together for good to those who love God, to those who are the called according to His purpose. (Romans 8:28)

LET US PRAY

I trust in You O Lord, let me never be ashamed.
Deliver me and protect me from (name your stressful situation) *for you are my strength.*

I will rejoice in Your mercy for You know all my problems and how much I have suffered.
I place all my trust in You and my life is in Your hand.

Save me from (name your stressful situation)
Do not let me be ashamed for I have placed all my trust in You.
(Adapted from Psalm 31)

ঌ6ঌ
TRANSFORM YOURSELF
(Renew your Mind)

Do not be conformed to this world, but be transformed by the renewing of your mind, that you may prove what is that good and acceptable and perfect will of God. (Romans 12:2)

Your thinking patterns which include your thoughts, beliefs, attitudes and mental imagery are so powerful that they can trigger the body's stress reaction just as well as a real event. These thoughts do not even have to be true for them to trigger the stress reaction or to increase the stress in your already stressful situation.

In situations where you are dealing with an actual stressful event, your thoughts about the event may even contribute more to how you feel and react to the actual stressful event than external things.

Two people may be caught up in a storm at sea. One may see a piece of wood floating and assume that it is a shark fin. This thought by itself is enough to aggravate his stress reaction. It can even make him despair and consider taking off his life jacked so that he does not prolong his dying process after he concludes that he cannot survive the storm and the sharks.

The other person may see the same piece of floating wood and decide that he will not panic even if it turns out to be a shark. He may remind himself of the countless stories he has heard of people surviving similar situations and decide that he will be one of them. Because of these thoughts, he will have the will and the strength to do whatever it takes to prolong his life even if it means clinging to his boat for days until help comes.

Therefore, as your thoughts influence your behavior, you have to monitor your thoughts and make sure that they do not conform to the negativity in your stressful situation or let the negativity of your stressful situation determine how you will think.,

BE TRANSFORMED BY RENEWING YOUR MIND

Instead of letting negative thoughts negatively influence your stressful situation, learn to be aware of them so that you can replace them with positive thoughts from the Word of God.

Renew your mind by meditating on Scripture and you will break the cycle in which negative thoughts contribute to increasing the stress in your already stressful situation and the resultant increased stress in turn generates more negative thoughts.

When any thoughts enter your mind, ask yourself if they fulfill the Bible's criteria of,
Whatever things are true,
Whatever things are noble,
Whatever things are just,
Whatever things are pure,
Whatever things are lovely,
Whatever things are of good report,
If there is any virtue
And if there is anything praiseworthy meditate on these things. (Philippians 4:8)

If your thoughts fall below this standard, then replace them with positive, power filled statements from the Bible which we will call **SWORD WORDS**.

SWORD WORDS

To effectively fight all the negative thoughts and temptations that may arise in your stressful situation, you have to use the **Sword of the Spirit, which is the word of God.** (Ephesians 6:17).

Emulate Jesus who used the Word of God to counter all the temptations of the devil when He was in the wilderness (Matthew 4). Whatever the devil suggested, He refuted by quoting Scripture.

Therefore, whenever negative thoughts assail you, find the appropriate **SWORD WORDS** and use them to defend and protect your mind. For example, if you are unemployed and are in dire need of money to buy medicine for your sick child and you find that negative thoughts such as "I will never get a job", "I will never get enough money to buy medicine",

"My child will never get well" keep crossing your mind, do not allow yourself to continue thinking on those lines.

Do not entertain those negative thoughts for if you concentrate on them, you will find that they will make you even more troubled, anxious and miserable than you already are. They will add to the distress you are already experiencing, demoralize you and may even plunge you into depression.

Instead of dwelling on these negative thoughts, whenever they sneak up on you replace them with, **God shall supply all your need according to His riches in glory by Christ Jesus.** (Philippians 4:19) Let these be the **SWORD WORDS** that you use to fight the negative thoughts and feelings attacking you.

Say them and believe them and after several repetitions you will find that you have a calm, sure and purposeful state of mind. You will be going forth doing your activities sure that God will supply all your needs. You don't have to know how He will do it, you only have to believe that He can and will do it.

If you are called for a job interview and your predominant thoughts are the negative ones, you will go looking depressed and acting desperate and this will reduce your chances of getting the job.

If you decide to make your **SWORD WORDS** your predominant thoughts and keep reminding yourself that **God shall supply all your need according to His riches in glory by Christ Jesus.** (Philippians 4:19) you will be relaxed and confident and this will increase your chances of getting the job.

WIELD YOUR SWORD WORDS

Therefore, regardless of your specific stressful situation, refuse to entertain any negative thoughts, feelings or temptations.

Go through your Bible and find the **SWORD WORDS** that are specific for your situation and then meditate on them until you eradicate the negative ones.

If for instance thoughts of your inadequacy cross your mind, slay them with **The people who know their God shall be strong, and carry out great exploits.** (Daniel 11:32)

When thoughts of incapability enter your mind, scatter them with **I can do all things through Christ who strengthens me.** (Philippians 4:13)

When thoughts of impossibility dock into your mind, drown them with **With God all things are possible.** (Matthew 19:26)

When thoughts of failure approach, repel them with **In all these things we are more than conquerors through Him who loved us.** (Romans 8:37)

When confusing thoughts pervade your mind nullify them with **God is not the author of confusion but of peace.** (1 Corinthians 14:33)

Whenever a strong temptation tries to floor you, stand on **God is faithful, who will not allow you to be tempted beyond what you are able, but with the temptation, will also make the way of escape, that you may be able to bear it.** (1 Corinthians 10:13)

If the negative thoughts and feelings are persistent, copy the relevant scriptures and carry them with you wherever you go so that you can refer to them and meditate on them be it in the bus, at work or as you drive back home.

DO NOT FEAR YOUR STORM

Fear is so detrimental to managing stress that fearful thoughts must be addressed separately. You must never be afraid of your stormy stressful situation. Do not fear the violent wind, the turbulent waves or the bloodthirsty predators.

Do not fear your storm because when you do, you torture yourself for **Fear involves torment** (1 John 4:18) and by entertaining fearful thoughts, you also terrorize yourself into submission and imprison yourself in your stressful situation.

Fear will detain you in your stressful situation using several means. It will distort your perception and the challenges will appear much bigger and more menacing than they really are. The odds will appear worse and the prognosis grimmer. It will petrify your creativity and you will be unable to visualize a way out. By freezing your mind, fear will have begun to bind you to your stressful situation.

Fear will also stifle your tongue and muffle your speech. It will make your tongue stick to the roof of your mouth and you will find yourself stammering instead of speaking up clearly to right your situation. By silencing you, fear will prolong your incarceration in your stressful situation.

Fear will further bind you by paralyzing your hands and legs. It will make you too scared to get up and do anything to help yourself. It will slowly but surely disable you as it moulds you into a cowardly creature that creeps in the shadows of life afraid to stand up in the light and fight for its rights.

By freezing your mind, stifling your tongue and paralyzing your hands, fear will have effectively locked you up in your stressful situation. Once fear has you under its terrible grip, it will not even need to hurt you to keep you restrained. By just suggesting or even creating illusions of what may happen to you if you try to end your stressful situation, the enemy will use your fear to weaken your resolve, sap your will to fight and therefore prolong your confinement to your stressful situation. You must therefore never, ever be afraid of your stormy stressful situation.

If fear has been imprisoning you, you can use the power that is in the Word of God to break free from its grip on your mind. Use your **SWORD WORDS** and free yourself **For God has not given us a spirit of fear, but of power and of love and of a sound mind.** (2 Timothy 1:7).

To effectively overcome your fearful thoughts using your **SWORD WORDS**, you also have to hold up your shield of faith because faith is the antidote of fear. Replace all fearful thoughts with your **SWORD WORDS** and then have faith that God will see you through your stressful situation.

When the disciples were caught up in their storm, Jesus asked them, **Why are you so fearful? How is it that you have no faith?** (Mark 4:40) He asked them this because if they had faith that Jesus was able to calm their storm, they would not have been afraid of it no matter how high the waves were rising, how strong the wind was blowing or how fast their boat was filling with water.

In the same way, whenever you begin to feel afraid of your storm, say to yourself, **The Lord is my helper; I will not fear** (Hebrews 13: 6) and let these be your **SWORD**

WORDS. Meditate on them certain that the Lord is going to help you and your fears will dissipate.

If as you try to leave your stressful situation, fear attempts to hold you back, say to yourself **Be strong and of good courage; do not be afraid, nor be dismayed, for the Lord your God is with you wherever you go.** (Joshua 1:9) Overcome the fearful thoughts with these **SWORD WORDS** and then step out in faith. Believe that the Lord is with you wherever you go and you will have no reason to fear the dangers that may be lurking on the wayside or the uncertainties waiting at your destination.

When people try to make you fear them, say to yourself **The Lord is the strength of my life; of whom shall I be afraid?** (Psalm 27:1) Defeat the fearful thoughts with these **SWORD WORDS,** have faith that Jesus will strengthen you and then go out to face them.

When frightful thoughts of how big, bad, dangerous, fatal, incurable or unconquerable the multitude of problems attacking you are, fight them with **Be strong, do not fear! Behold, your God will come with vengeance, with the recompense of God; He will come and save you.** (Isaiah 35:4) Crush the fearful thoughts with these **SWORD WORDS,** have faith that God will aid you, save you and avenge you then set out to solve your problems.

Therefore, irrespective of your specific situation, there are **SWORD WORDS** to fight all fears. Go through your Bible and memorize the **SWORD WORDS** that you will need to free your mind from fear and then have faith that God will strengthen you as you stand up and free your body from your oppressive stressful situation.

DO NOT GIVE UP

When you begin this battle to emancipate your mind from all negative thoughts, feelings and temptations, they may seem to overwhelm you due to their numbers and how rapidly they keep entering your mind. But, do not give up. Persist and tear them down with your **SWORD WORDS** one at a time. The pace may seem slow initially but with prayer, practice, patience and persistence, you will become adept at wielding your **SWORD WORDS**.

As you persist, you will find that the more familiar you become with the Scriptures, the less the negative thoughts will be able to oppress you for you will have the positive Biblical truths filling your mind, flooding your heart and rolling from your tongue.

Therefore, diligently work with your **SWORD WORDS** to ensure that you have been **Transformed by the renewing of your mind, that you may prove what is that good and acceptable and perfect will of God** (Romans 12:2) so that you can set out to position yourself.

ACTION PLAN

1. Write down all the negative thoughts, feelings and temptations that beset you. Go through your Bible and write down the **SWORD WORDS** that you will use to counter them.

Copy your **SWORD WORDS** on a paper and carry them with you wherever you go so that you can meditate on them and repeat them to yourself as often as necessary.

LET US PRAY

Let the words of my mouth and the meditation of my heart be acceptable in Your sight, O Lord, my strength and my Redeemer. (Psalm 19:14)

7

POSITION YOURSELF
(Work Physically)

Thus says the Lord to you: "Do not be afraid nor dismayed because of this great multitude, for the battle is not yours, but God's. Tomorrow go down against them. …Position yourselves, stand still and see the salvation of the Lord, who is with you." (2 Chronicles 20: 15-17)

After you have transformed your mind with the Word of God and you are now better able to determine what is that good and acceptable and perfect will of God for you in your situation, you now have to take up your position in the battlefield just as King Jehoshaphat and the people of Judah did. (2 Chronicles 20)

To position yourself is to put yourself in the most advantageous place in your situation by taking the steps of faith that you know would be pleasing and acceptable to God. It is doing the best that you can with whatever resources that you still have left so as to ensure that you are in the best possible state to receive and maximize His blessings.

If you are alone in your boat lost at sea, bandage your wounds, mend your oars, fix your mast and patch your sails. Do what you can to help yourself so that when the Lord shows you the direction to row your boat, you will be ready to move at once.

If you have a physical illness, pray for yourself, go to healing services, consult a doctor, take your medications faithfully and eat healthily. Put yourself in the state where you are most able to receive God's blessing of total healing as the doctors treat you.

If your business is not doing well, pray for it, show up every day, remit your tithes and taxes faithfully, improve your pricing, products and services as you ethically position your business the best way you can in the online or offline marketplace.

If you are unemployed, pray for a job, send out application letters, update your skills, use your talents to generate money and volunteer your services.

Do not spend the whole day lying in bed feeling sorry for yourself even if your circumstances have changed drastically and you now have to use the bus instead of your BMW. Do what you can with what you have to position yourself where you are best able to increase your chances of getting a job or creating one for yourself.

If you are lying by the Pool of Bethesda, (John 5:1-8) and you really want to be healed, take up your position at the edge of the Pool so that you will be the first person to get in when the angel stirs the water.

Even if you are too sick to walk and there is nobody to carry you, crawl to the poolside so that you will be able to fall in immediately it is stirred.

Therefore, regardless of how sick you are or how many other ailing people are also waiting for the angel, you have to do what you can to position yourself in the best way possible.

Look for a way to position yourself strategically and not for excuses. In this way, you will not have to suffer for 38 years in your stressful situation like the sick man by the Pool of Bethesda as you wait for a solution to your situation.

In conclusion, remember that it does not matter what type of stressful situation you may be in right now because once you have done the spiritual work of praying and trusting God and then done the mental wok of transforming your mind with the Word of God, you now have to step out in faith to do the physical work of positioning yourself in the place where you are most likely to receive a solution to your stressful situation.

STAND STILL

After you have positioned yourself, and done all that you can, you now have to stand still and wait on the Lord.

You are to stand still and continue standing in your position even if the winds of adversity and waves of misfortune are still pounding on you.

To be able to stand still and hold your ground even under harsh conditions, you have to:
1. Put on the whole armor of God
2. Look up to Jesus and not at your stressful situation
3. Look up to Jesus and not at the people stressing you

PUT ON THE WHOLE ARMOR OF GOD

Finally, my brethren, be strong in the Lord and in the power of His might.

Put on the whole armor of God, that you may be able to stand against the wiles of the devil.

For we do not wrestle against flesh and blood, but against principalities, against powers, against the rulers of the darkness of this age, against spiritual hosts of wickedness in the heavenly places.

Therefore take up the whole armor of God, that you may be able to withstand in the evil day, and having done all, to stand.

Stand therefore, having girded your waist with truth,

having put on the breastplate of righteousness,

and having shod your feet with the preparation of the gospel of peace;

above all, taking the shield of faith with which you will be able to quench all the fiery darts of the wicked one.

And take the helmet of salvation,

and the sword of the Spirit which is the Word of God;

praying always with all prayer and supplication in the Spirit,

being watchful to this end with all perseverance and supplication for all the saints. (Ephesians 6:10-18)

To be able to stand in your position, you have to put on your whole armor for in some stressful situations, you may have to battle wicked spiritual powers in the heavenly places. In those situations, you will have to have the whole armor on in order to be able to resist the attacks of the devil and remain standing in your position.

Therefore, ensure that you have let the Lord Jesus into your heart and confess Him as your Savior (**helmet of salvation**).

Make sure that you are firmly rooted in the Word of God by reading it (**Gospel of peace boots**), living it and speaking it (**the sword of the spirit**).

Be truthful (**belt of truth**), live right (**breastplate of righteousness**) and pray at all times.

Most importantly, believe God and hold firmly onto your faith (**shield of faith**) all the time and you will be able to defeat all the attacks of the devil.

LOOK TO JESUS NOT YOUR SITUATION

To remain standing in your strategic position, even when your situation is still very stressful, you have to look up to Jesus from where your help will come from and not at your situation from where your stress is coming from.

Set your inner focus or the eyes of your mind on Jesus, His power, mercy and faithfulness.

Keep your eyes on God and learn from David in 1 Samuel chapter 17 when he was faced with the challenge of fighting Goliath. Goliath was over nine feet tall, his armor weighed over 120 pounds (60 kilograms) and the iron head of his spear weighed over 14 pounds (7 kilograms).

He wore a bronze helmet, his legs were protected by a bronze armor, and he carried a bronze javelin slung over his shoulder.

If David had focused on these facts, the reflection from Goliath's metallic armor would have blinded him with fear to the great power of God and he may have concluded that there was no way on earth that he could defeat Goliath and therefore given up and not even tried like the other soldiers.

Instead, David focused on the immense power and protection of God that He had experienced while tending his sheep. He focused on the fact that if God was able to help him kill lions and bears, surely He was also able to help him defeat Goliath.

Likewise, do not concentrate on all the bad things that the Goliath in your stressful situation has done to you, is doing to you or is threatening to do to you. Instead, concentrate on what God can do to the Goliath in your situation.

The fact that David did not focus on Goliath does not mean that he ignored Goliath. He saw him, the whole nine feet encased in bronze armor. He acknowledged the facts of the gigantic challenge that he was facing and the consequences of losing but then he returned the focus of his attention to what he knew and believed about God.

Therefore, be aware of your stressful situation, what has gone wrong and what the possible solutions (if any) are. Analyze the facts, position yourself in the best way possible and then remind yourself that **With God all things are possible** (Matthew 19:26).

Do this and you will be able to achieve what is seemingly humanly impossible as your attitude changes from one of being hopelessly defeated to one of being divinely assisted.

Goliath challenged the Israelites every morning and evening for forty days. The daily intimidation and tormenting of the Israelite army by Goliath may have contributed to the Israelite soldiers feeling totally outdone and hopeless.

Therefore, once you are aware of all the facts and figures pertaining to your stressful situation, do not keep going over them time and time again. Do not remind yourself every morning that it has been seven years, three months and two days since you separated from your spouse.

Do not remind yourself every evening of how fast your viral load is rising.

Do not remind yourself every day of how many organs your cancer has metastasized to.

Do not keep telling yourself that the Goliath that you are facing has never been defeated before. Instead, remind yourself everyday that **With God all things are possible.** (Matthew 19:26)

There were also many other odds which were against David winning his battle against Goliath. These included his inexperience, as he was just a youthful shepherd while Goliath was a man of war from his youth. There was also the fact that if David lost to Goliath the Israelites would have had to become servants of the Philistines. David did not dwell on these facts, all he did was to focus on what he knew deep down inside about God's ability.

Therefore, learn from David and do not concentrate on all the odds that are stacked against you and your seemingly powerlessness over them as this will convince you that you cannot triumph over your stressful situation.

Instead focus on the great advantage that you have which is having God on your side.

Even if the disease is still progressing, the bills piling and the child plunging more and more into drugs, believe that you can still win because God is able to make you win. He is able to restore your health, your family, your finances and whatever else is ailing in your life.

Therefore do not give up on yourself and on your situation without taking into consideration what God can do for you and for your situation.

LOOKING TO JESUS AND NOT AT PEOPLE

As you try to stand firmly in your position, you may encounter people who do not want you to stand at all. They may be doing their level best to keep you down and distressed.

Do not look at these people and concentrate on all the bad things that they are doing or saying to you.

Even if they are physically present in your strategic position, ignore them by focusing the eyes of your mind on Jesus. Look up to Jesus for strength, support, encouragement, validation and vindication.

Look up to Jesus to provide you with everything that you need to remain standing in your strategic position regardless of whether you are still being stressed by underminers, ostracizers, enablers or condemners.

Underminers

These are the people who are doing their level best to ensure that whatever you do fails. They may have hurt you badly in the past when they knocked you down and left you for dead and now that by the grace of God you have been able to drag yourself up, they want to see you floored again.

Learn to keep your attention focused on Jesus and not on them. Stand in your position being certain that whatever He has planned for you in your life will come to pass regardless of their actions.

You may not be able to stop their evil plans, hurting words or undermining actions but you can ask for His strength and protection so that you can continue standing in spite of it all.

Cry out to Him as King Jehoshaphat did when he prayed: **O our God, will You not judge them? For we have no power against this great multitude that is coming against us; nor do we know what to do, but our eyes are upon You.** (2 Chronicles 20:12)

Keep your eyes on Jesus and let Him strengthen you when you feel too weak to take their blows for He says **My grace is sufficient for you, for My strength is made perfect in weakness**. (2 Corinthians 12:9)

Let Him judge them for as the psalmist says: **But You have seen, for You observe trouble and grief, to repay it by Your hand. The helpless commits himself to You; You are the helper of the fatherless.** (Psalm 10:14) Let Him also punish them. Even if you can avenge yourself, do not retaliate. Leave it to God for he says **Vengeance is mine, I will repay.** (Hebrews 10: 30)

Ostracizers

These are the people who may be treating you like you are an unwanted member of society because of the disease that you are suffering from, the change in your financial and social status or for whatever other excuse they may have to shun you. They will want you to receive their negative perception of you, to believe it and then to live it.

Do not receive it, believe it or begin living as they want you to. Do not be molded by their expectations, ridicule or bigotry.

Do not change your speech and behavior to agree with the negative image that they have of you and that they are trying to project onto you. Do not start saying words or doing things to suit them and to show that you accept that you are a lesser human being just because of the changes that you are going through as a result of your stressful situation.

Look up to Jesus for your validation and not at their demeaning innuendos, words and actions even if they are church going people.

Base your security and significance on His love for you. Reaffirm in yourself who you are according to the Word of God and with this firm assurance you will not need others to validate you and you will be able to dismiss their devaluation.

Remind yourself every day that you are a valuable child of God and that He loves you regardless of your situation in life. Focus and draw from His love for you so that you can continue standing firmly and securely in your position.

Enablers

These are the people who like to see you wallowing in your misery and going back to your problems time and again like **A dog returns to his own vomit and a sow having washed, to her wallowing in the mire.** (2 Peter 2:22).

These enablers may not be comfortable with relating with the new you if you clean up your act and manage your stressful situation once and for all. They may be telling you that your situation is hopeless or that you are useless and will remain permanently trapped by your problems.

They will discourage and deter you from standing firm. They will taunt you mercilessly if you totter even once.

Do not fear to take a new stand in your life because of what people will say if you should slip back into your old habits. Ignore such people and learn to look up to Jesus and His Word for strength and encouragement to keep standing firmly in your position. He is the only one who really knows how hard you are trying to stand and hold your ground in the face of all the tricks, temptations and attacks.

Should you slip and sin, ask Him to forgive you, forgive yourself and then take up your position once again.

Do not fear to serve God in word and deed because of what the people who know you now or those who knew the old you will say if you should sin. Be sincere in your attempt to live a pure life and ignore them for in the final analysis, when all is said and done, it is only His opinion that will matter.

Condemners

These are the people who insist on stoning you with their words and deeds even after you have confessed your sins, been forgiven by Jesus, done your time and repaid whatever damage you could.

They do not want you or anyone else to forget the sins that you committed in your past. They want you to grovel on the ground in your guilt for the rest of your life.

Do not let anyone chain you to your forgiven sins. Do not receive condemnation from anyone as we have all sinned for the Bible says **All we like sheep have gone astray; We have turned, every one, to his own way.** (Isaiah 53:6)

Therefore, anytime anyone tries to make your feel guilty, remind yourself that **There is therefore now no condemnation to those who are in Christ Jesus.** (Romans 8:1). Do not receive condemnation from anyone whether it is your family, friends or even from yourself in the form of self-accusing thoughts.

Look up to Jesus and receive his gift of forgiveness. Let His blood wash away the sins, guilt and remorse from your mind and spirit once and for all. Dry your tears with the towel of self forgiveness and then stand firmly in your position and sin no more.

ACTION PLAN

1. To help you position yourself in the best way possible in your stressful situation answer the following questions
a. Am I praying without ceasing for my stressful situation?

b. Have I consulted specialist to help me deal with my stressful situation?
These can be doctors, counselors, the job vacancies section of the newspapers or even workshops.

c. Have I done what the specialists recommend?
This can include taking medication, stopping smoking, being less argumentative with your spouse, taking your child to a drug rehabilitation center, updating your skills or improving your products' packaging.

2. Copy Ephesians 6:10-18 and hang it where you can see it every morning to remind you to put on your armor of God before you head out to position yourself.

PUT ON THE WHOLE ARMOR OF GOD

Finally, my brethren, be strong in the Lord and in the power of His might.

Put on the whole armor of God, that you may be able to stand against the wiles of the devil.

For we do not wrestle against flesh and blood, but against principalities, against powers, against the rulers of the darkness of this age, against spiritual hosts of wickedness in the heavenly places.

Therefore take up the whole armor of God, that you may be able to withstand in the evil day, and having done all, to stand.

Stand therefore, having girded your waist with truth, having put on the breastplate of righteousness, and having shod your feet with the preparation of the gospel of peace; above all, taking the shield of faith with which you will be able to quench all the fiery darts of the wicked one. And take the helmet of salvation, and the sword of the Spirit which is the Word of God; praying always with all prayer and supplication in the Spirit, being watchful to this end with all perseverance and supplication for all the saints. (Ephesians 6:10-18)

LET US PRAY

Where will my help come from?

My help will come from the Lord,
Who made heaven and earth.
He will not allow my foot to be moved;
He who keeps me will not sleep.
Behold, He who keeps (insert your name here) *shall neither sleep nor slumber.*

The Lord is my keeper;
The Lord is my shade at my right hand.
The sun shall not harm me during the day, nor the moon at night.
The Lord shall protect me from all evil,
He shall preserve my soul.
The Lord shall guard my going out and my coming in from this time forth, and even forevermore. (Adapted from Psalm 121)

8

WAIT ON THE LORD
(Be Patient)

Wait on the Lord; be of good courage, and he shall strengthen your heart; wait, I say, on the Lord. (Psalm 27:14)

After you have positioned yourself and you are standing in your position, you are now to wait for the Lord to provide you with whatever you have been praying for whether it is deliverance, healing, restoration or a breakthrough.

You are to stand and wait for Him to bring it to pass at His appointed time. Since His timing may be totally different from yours, you have to learn to **Rest in the Lord, and wait patiently for Him.** (Psalm 37: 7)

Rest by relaxing in the Lord and surrendering your urgency. Let go of the need to have your situation resolve when you want it to and in the manner that you would like it to. You have done all that you can, so now leave it to the Lord to do His will in His own time.

As you do so, trust His timing implicitly because this is the secret to waiting patiently. Acknowledge that He knows best and that He is always on time. Once you do this, you will not be restless and impatient because you know that He is never late and His judgments are never wrong. You will then be able to continue waiting patiently even if you do not see any tangible progress because you have the patience of hope and you believe Him when He says, **They shall not be ashamed who wait for Me.** (Isaiah 49: 23)

If you wake up feeling that your storm is taking too long to calm down, resist the temptation to hurry and row before He has showed you the direction you are to row your boat. Do not rush ahead of God for the results will be disastrous. If you are waiting on God to provide you with confirmation for a spouse or a business venture, wait for Him no matter how fast the opportunities and the years seem to be flying past you for He has His reasons for what may appear as a delay to you.

On the days when the wait may seem harder to bear, ask for grace to hold on until the end of that day. Pray for strength to pull through the day you are facing. Do not think or wonder how you will face tomorrow, next week or next month. Just pray as He taught **Give us this day our daily bread** (Matthew 6:11) and not "Give us this day bread for today and tomorrow" **For tomorrow will worry about its own things. Sufficient for the day is its own trouble.** (Matthew 6:34).

Therefore, pray for just what you need to sustain you through that day. If it is perseverance, strength or peace that you need to keep waiting patiently, ask for enough to sustain you to the end of that one day.

At the end of the day, before you go to sleep, thank Him for enabling you to pull through that day.

When you wake up the next morning, ask Him afresh for what you need to make it through that new day. In this way, you will be better able to live through your waiting period however long it may last if you break it down to 24 hour periods that each comprise of 8 hours of sleep.

Even if you have been diagnosed with a terminal illness, your life will be more manageable if you view it as sequential 24 hour stretches of time, rather than if you view it as one long stretch of time full of uncertainties.

Therefore face your waiting period one day at a time and remember that **The Lord is good to those who wait for Him, to the soul who seeks Him. It is good that one should hope and wait quietly for the salvation of the Lord.** (Lamentations 3:25-26)

TSUNAMIED!

Sometimes just after you have eased into your waiting period, that is when the tsunami hits you. Just as you begin to think that the worst is behind you, that is when you are tsunamied!

The night suddenly begins to get darker. It gets so dark that you can feel the darkness as it rests on your skin. The winds begin to howl and then the tsunami strikes!

The waves hit your boat with renewed ferocity and it is filling with water at an alarming rate. The wind flips it and you are ruthlessly tossed back into the water. As you try to come up for air, you are slammed back in by violent waves.

You are hemorrhaging seriously as the tsunami has ripped apart the remaining pieces of your life. It is at this point that you can identify with the disciples when they were caught up in their storm and they cried out to Jesus saying, **Teacher, do You not care that we are perishing?** (Mark 4:38)

So how do you deal with those dark, dismal and distressing days when the tsunami strikes before you have even recovered from the first storm? How do you cope when the plank that you had been painfully clinging onto for so long snaps and you are now about to drown in your problems?

What do you do when as you are waiting for God to restore your failing health your heart is broken? What do you do when as you are waiting for Him to restore your floundering finances, your family breaks up? What do you do when just as you are beginning to adjust to your spouse's death you discover that your last born is HIV positive?

There are three things that you can learn from Psalm 78 about what not to do during the darkest hour of your stormy stressful situation.
1. Do not speak against God
2. Do not test God
3. Do not break His commandments

DO NOT SPEAK AGAINST GOD

Yes, they spoke against God: They said, Can God prepare a table in the wilderness? Behold, He struck the rock, so that the waters gushed out, and the streams overflowed. Can He give bread also? Can He provide meat for His people? (Psalm 78:19-20)

Do not speak against God. Do not murmur against God. This is the time that you need God the most and so do not let the devil drive a wedge between you and God by encouraging you to **Curse God and die!** (Job 2:9) Instead be like Job who after all he suffered, **Did not sin with his lips.** (Job 2:10)

DO NOT TEST GOD

And they tested God in their heart by asking for the food of their fancy. (Psalm 78:18)

Do not deliberately put God to the test. Do not challenge God by saying "If you are really God, then get me out of this situation." or "If you are really that powerful then stop the tsunami right now" because He is able to do all things and He does not have to prove it to you.

Do not also question God saying, "I know that you were able to solve that crisis last year, but are You able to solve this one?" because as Jesus said, **You shall not tempt the Lord your God.** (Matthew 4:7)

DO NOT BREAK HIS COMMANDMENTS

Yet they tested and provoked the Most High God, and did not keep His testimonies, but turned back and acted unfaithfully like their fathers; They were turned aside like a deceitful bow. For they provoked Him to anger with their high places, and moved Him to jealousy with their carved images. When God heard this, He was furious. (Psalm 78:56-59)

Do not be like the Israelites who broke the commandments and made the Lord furious. This is not the time to sin by assuming that your sins will be exonerated on account of the massive stresses that you are going through. God still expects you to be loyal and obey His commandments and not to rebel against Him.

Therefore, do not anger him by turning to other gods to provide a solution for your stressful situation. Do not look to palmistry, witchcraft, horoscopes, consult a psychic or medium or do any other thing that He has forbidden with the hope that it will help you out of your stressful situation **For it is written, "You shall worship the Lord your God, and Him only you shall serve."** (Matthew 4:10)

Instead of speaking against God or testing Him or breaking His commandments after you have been tsunamied, what you must do is:
1. Remind yourself of God's faithfulness in the past
2. Remind yourself that the battle is not yours but God's
3. Hope in the Lord always

REMEMBER GOD'S FAITHFULNESS

When we read about all what God did for the Israelites we are amazed at how quickly they forgot.

From the book of Exodus, we see that God did extraordinary things for the Israelites when they were slaves in Egypt so that Pharaoh would free them. He turned rivers into blood. He sent swarms of flies and plagued them with locusts and frogs. He destroyed cattle and grapevines with hail, trees with frost and killed all the firstborns of the Egyptians.

Once they were free, He continued to do great things for them and to show them His power.
He divided the Red Sea and they were able to pass through it without drowning. In the daytime, He led them with a cloud and at night with a light of fire. He caused manna to rain from heaven and they ate the food of angels to their satisfaction.

But when they were faced with a challenge, they were asking if God could prepare a table in the wilderness for them!!

Sometimes we are not much different from the Israelites when we are faced by a stressful situation and especially one that has persisted for a long time. We forget so easily the good times when we encounter bad times. We concentrate on the current stressful situation so much that our blessings retreat into the recesses of our minds and become some insignificant background features.

We can recount all the bad things that have been happening to us but when someone asks us to recall just one good thing that the Lord has done for us, we can't remember any. We seem to develop a special type of memory loss where we forget all the good and remember only the bad.

Therefore, when you find your faith, hope and trust in God wavering after you have been hit by the tsunami, take the time to remind yourself of how God has manifested His love, power and faithfulness to you in the past.

How Many Times?

How many times has God freed you from other difficult situations?
How many times has He protected you when you were in danger?
How many times has He showed you the way when you were totally clueless?
How many times has He opened the windows of heaven and blessed you with the best?
How many times has He parted your problems enabling you to live unhindered by them?

How many times has He made rivers of abundance flow into your parched life?

Go through your **GOD IS FAITHFUL** notebook and remind yourself of all the good things God has done for you. Read it often to bring back to your mind all the wonderful ways He manifested His power in your life. Let them serve as proof that He is still able to do great things for you today right there in the middle of your stormy stressful situation.

In addition, tell yourself that if God gave you that big blessing last year, then He can still bless you again and restore your marriage, rebuild your finances, heal your body and resolve whatever stressful situation you may be facing today for He is still the same great God. Let the great things that God has done for you in the past console you and encourage you to keep waiting patiently for Him to do other great things in your life today and tomorrow.

Read your **GOD IS FAITHFUL** notebook every time you feel discouraged until His miraculous works are etched into your mind. Carry them in your heart like David who carried the evidence of God's faithfulness with him wherever he went such that when he was faced with the unexpected challenge of fighting Goliath, he was able to testify before all that **The Lord, who delivered me from the paw of the lion and from the paw of the bear, He will deliver me from the hand of this Philistine.** (1 Samuel 17:37)

If you do this, and carry the evidence of God's faithfulness and goodness in your heart, it does not matter how stormy your situation may get, for your days will not be consumed by futility nor your years by fear of the enemy.

REMEMBER THE BATTLE IS NOT YOURS

When King Jehoshaphat and the people of Judah felt overwhelmed by the large armies that were attacking them, the Lord said to them, **Do not be afraid nor dismayed because of this great multitude, for the battle is not yours, but God's.** (2 Chronicles 20:15).

The Lord God was going to fight the battle for them because they were unable to fight it for themselves as the armies attacking them were too strong for them.

Likewise, when your problems overwhelm and threaten to overpower you, remind yourself that **The battle is not yours, but God's** (2 Chronicles 20:15) and let Him fight it for you. Give it up to God and wait for Him to fight it for you. You do not give up, you give it up to God. You give Him the battle so that He can fight it for you.

Realize as Paul did when they were faced with very many problems in Asia that it was a good thing that their burdens were too heavy for them to bear because then they had no choice but to entrust themselves and their burdens to God.

They therefore gave them up to the One who was bigger than them. The One who was also able to raise them from the dead if their burdens killed them. **For we do not want you to be ignorant, brethren, of our trouble which came to us in Asia: that we were burdened beyond measure, above strength, so that we despaired even of life. Yes, we had the sentence of death in ourselves, that we should not trust in ourselves but in God who raises the dead, who delivered us from so great a death, and does deliver us; in whom we trust that He will still deliver us.** (2 Corinthians 1: 8-10)

Therefore, believe that God can deliver you from all your problems and do not limit His power to help you in your stressful situation with your unbelief. Keep your faith in Him firm and you will find that you can wait with the confidence that you will triumph over your stressful situation because the outcome of your crisis does not depend on your inability to solve the problems but rather, it depends on God's ability to solve them for you.

HOPE IN THE LORD ALWAYS

You must always hope in the Lord even when your skies and sea have turned black and you cannot see your way out of your situation. Do not give up and lose hope no matter how long the winds of adversity and waves of misfortune have been pounding on you.

Do not give up no matter how many times you have tried and failed to leave the shark infested waters. Do not let the waves of hopelessness overwhelm you even if the waters are up to your neck and it seems that you are just about to sink.

Do not give up or give in to despair, for once these feelings of hopelessness overwhelm you, you will find that all the other negative emotions that you had defeated will resurface and re-attack you. Fears that you had overcome will reappear and paralyze you once again. Doubts that you had quelled will return, now masquerading as undisputable certainties.

You must therefore always remain hopeful for hope enables you to look beyond your present stressful situation to the possibility of a better tomorrow.

Establish your hope firmly in Jesus even when humanly there seems to be no reason to hope for He is able to calm your storm just as He was able to calm the storm in which the disciples were caught in when **He arose and rebuked the wind, and said to the sea, "Peace be still!" And the wind ceased and there was a great calm.** (Mark 4:39)

Learn also from the woman in Mark 5:25-29 who had suffered terribly from severe bleeding for twelve years. She did not lose hope even though she had spent all her money consulting doctor and yet her condition kept getting worse.

She still had hope that she could be healed and that is the reason she bothered to press through the crowd to touch the hem of Jesus' garment.

Her faith in Jesus' healing power made her well but it was her hope that she could still be healed that enabled her to press through the crowd.

Therefore, do not give up on Jesus regardless of how long the stormy stressful situation has persisted in your life or how many consultants have been unable to help you or how complicated it has become.

Do not lose your hope in God even if there seems to be no earthly reason for you to hope for **Hope that is seen is not hope; for why does one still hope for what he sees? But if we hope for what we do not see, we eagerly wait for it with perseverance.** (Romans 8: 24-25)

PHYSICALLY DYING AS YOU WAIT

In some stressful situations, you may find that your physical health is deteriorating at a very fast rate. You may have come to the realization that your physical death is more of a proximal certainty rather than a distal eventuality.

Do not be distraught for everyone will eventually die, it is just a matter of when, for **To everything there is a season, a time for every purpose under heaven: a time to be born, and a time to die** (Ecclesiastes 3:1-2)

Instead, be consoled by the fact that if you die after you have accepted Jesus Christ as your Savior, you can look forward to stress free eternal life.

Count the fact that you have discovered that you have limited time on this earth as a blessing in disguise. This is because there are many people who will die on the same day with you and some of them will not be expecting it. As a result, they will neither have primed themselves to meet their Creator nor will they have prepared their families and friends.

Since you have the opportunity to prepare for your departure, make good use of it and begin to by making peace with God and laying some treasures in Heaven.

If you are not saved, get saved (see chapter on Let Jesus In). Ask God to show you any unfinished Kingdom business that He wants you to undertake before your departure.

Then use the time that you have left to sort out your affairs here on earth. Write your will. Let your family and friends know who you want to take care of your progeny and property. You do not have to tell your preteens that you are about to die if you do not feel comfortable telling them as yet, but you can begin to prepare them.

Prepare your children by grounding them in the Lord through daily prayer and Bible reading.

Encourage them to develop a personal relationship with Jesus Christ and urge the older ones who can comprehend what that means to get saved.

Emphasize the importance of being responsible and taking responsibility for their lives. Give them examples of people who made mistakes and had to pay heavy prices for them so that they can begin to make wise choices even when they are all alone.

Talk to them about their future career choices and other life choices. If you have time and the means consider making videos that they can watch even when you will not be there and hear your voice once again.

Teach them how to save and live economically within their means. Consider opening bank accounts for the older ones.

Show them how to shop for nutritious foods.

Instruct them on how to express themselves clearly when they go to the doctor.

Do whatever you can to guide them now that you have the chance so as to ensure that they will not only survive but also thrive when you will not be there to take care of them.

ACTION PLAN

1. Every day jot three things you are grateful for in your **GOD IS FAITHFUL** notebook and carry it with you to read and remind yourself how God has been good to you every time you feel you can't take the stress anymore.

2. Describe the following in your **GOD IS FAITHFUL** notebook:
a. 10 situations when God freed you from other problematic situations
b. 10 situations in which God protected you when you were in danger
c. 10 situations in which God showed you the way when you were totally clueless
d. 10 situations in which God opened the windows of heaven and blessed you with the best
e. 10 situations in which God parted your problems enabling you to live unhindered by them
f. 10 situations in which God made rivers of abundance flow into your parched life

LET US PRAY

Hear my prayer O Lord and listen to my supplications.
In Your faithfulness answer me and hear my prayer.

I will remember the days of old
I will think about all Your works.
I will ponder on the work of Your hands.
I spread out my hands to You.

My soul longs for You like a thirsty land. Answer me O Lord and deliver me from (name your stressful situation). *I will wait on You O Lord, for You are my God.* (Adapted from Psalm 143)

MEDICAL RELAXATION TECHNIQUES

When facing a protracted and stressful waiting period, you will cope with it better if you incorporate medical techniques into your lifestyle. To do so, ensure that you:
1. Breathe
2. Meditate
3. Visualize
4. Exercise
5. Eat
6. Sleep
7. Get a massage

ABDOMINAL BREATHING

Abdominal breathing or diaphragmatic breathing or deep breathing is one of the fastest and easiest way to counter act the body's stress response.

Abdominal breathing has been found to be effective in reducing muscle tension and heart rates which increase when someone is stresses.

It has also been found to be beneficial in the management of stress related headaches, fatigue and panic attacks.

Abdominal breathing is a very simple relaxation technique as all you have to do is to loosen your clothing, lie down in a quiet and place your hand on your abdomen.

Take a deep breath through your nose until you feel your abdomen rising, hold your breath for a few seconds and then exhale completely until your abdomen falls. Repeat several times and you will begin to feel relaxed.

If you are not able to lie down, you can also breathe deeply while standing up or sitting down as it is also a discrete relaxation technique that can be practiced at anytime and in any place whenever and wherever stress strikes whether in the office or at home or in a traffic jam or in the middle of an argument.

Therefore, always take several deep breaths whenever you begin to feel stressed and you will be able to manage the situation more calmly.

CHRISTIAN MEDITATION

Meditation is another very effective relaxation technique.

For those who are not familiar with mediation, to meditate is simply to focus your attention on one thought.

Research has shown that meditation lowers the heart rate, respiratory rate and muscle tension which are all increased during the body's stress reaction. Consequently, by mediating one counters the stress reaction and is able to relax.

Therefore, choose a Scripture that speaks to your stressful situation and meditate on it every day. For example, if your problems are intimidating you, you can choose to meditate on **I can do all things through Christ who strengthens me** (Philippians 4:13)

If your stressful situation is telling you that your problem is impossible and no one can help you, choose to meditate on **With God all things are possible.** (Matthew 19:26)

After you have chosen your Scripture, lie down in a quiet place and give it your complete attention. Ponder it until you feel its truth percolating your entire being.

If your mind wanders to your problems, gently bring it back to your Scripture by repeating it until it fills your mind.

You can meditate in the morning before you head out to position yourself so as to strengthen and encourage yourself.

Or, you can also meditate in the evening before you sleep to calm down and get a good night's sleep.

Or, you can even do it twice a day which is even better because regardless of when you choose to meditate, ensure you meditate regularly so as to reap more benefits since its effects are cumulative.

Therefore schedule at least 10 minutes each day to meditate your stress away.

Aside from the medical and physical benefits of meditating on the Word of God, there are also spiritual benefits for the Bible tells us that **Blessed is the man who ☐ his delight is in the law of the Lord, and in His law he meditates day and night. He shall be like a tree planted by the rivers of water, that brings forth its fruit in its season, whose leaf also shall not wither and whatever he does shall prosper.** (Psalm 1:1-3)

Therefore, consistently meditate on the Word of God so that you are well grounded in it and become like a deeply rooted tree planted by rivers. These rivers of living water which you constantly draw up into yourself by meditating on the Word, will provide you with abundant sustenance.

You will be continually nourished by the nurturing Word of God and your flowers or projects will bud and blossom to bring forth fruit at your God appointed season.

Your leaf or hope shall not wither no matter how stressful your situation may be because you will always have a Word to refresh and rejuvenate you. Your hope for a better tomorrow will not wilt and die because there is power surging through your veins from the life giving Word that you are firmly rooted in.

CHRISTIAN VISUALIZATION

Visualization or guided imagery is another effective stress management technique. It is also an enjoyable one since it involves imagining yourself out of the stressful situation.

Therefore, schedule time each day to imagine yourself stress free using all your 5 senses – namely sight, sound, smell, touch and taste.

For example if "stress free" for you means lounging on a beach with billions in the bank, close your eyes and
a. see (with your mind's eye) the expansive blue sea sprawling in front of you as the sun smiles on it
b. hear the waves lapping on the beach
c. smell the fresh sea air and the crisp bank notes you have just withdrawn
e. touch the cool glass with your drink
d. taste the tantalizing tropical coconut drink
f. feel the tension and stress evaporating from your mind.

You can also use Bible verses for Christian visualization. A perfect example is Psalm 23.
The LORD *is* my shepherd; I shall not want.

He makes me to lie down in green pastures;

He leads me beside the still waters.

He restores my soul;

He leads me in the paths of righteousness for His name's sake.

Yea, though I walk through the valley of the shadow of death, I will fear no evil;

For You *are* with me;

Your rod and Your staff, they comfort me.

You prepare a table before me in the presence of my enemies;

You anoint my head with oil;

My cup runs over.

Surely goodness and mercy shall follow me all the days of my life;

And I will dwell in the house of the LORD Forever.

Therefore, to use Psalm 23 for visualization,
a. see yourself lying on a picnic blanket in a lush green lawn
b. hear the calm stream rippling gently nearby and the birds chirping in the background
c. smell the oil He has used to anoint your head and the rose bushes nearby
d. touch the deluxe picnic hamper He has set before you
e. taste the delicacies He has prepared for you
f. feel the Lord comforting you and your soul being restored as fear and anxiety leave and goodness and mercy begin following you.

You can choose your own different Scriptures that are relevant to your current stressful situation to help you visualize the scenarios that make you feel relaxed.
Consider taping your own visualization relaxation tapes.

EXERCISE REGULARLY

You have to exercise regularly because physical exercise is a very effective relaxation technique. All three groups of exercises, that is aerobic exercises, stretching exercises and weight bearing exercises are helpful in managing stress. They also result in the release of endorphins by the body which makes you feel good.

AEROBIC EXERCISES

Aerobic exercises are especially beneficial because they result in a reduction of the circulating stress hormones produced by the body during a stressful event. When you are unable to use them up by fighting your stressors or fleeing from your stressful situation, they accumulate in the body and contribute to the development of stress related diseases.

By engaging in aerobic activities such as running, walking briskly, playing football, basketball, swimming, walking up stairs or gardening, you are able to constructively 'work them out' of your body.

Therefore, work out aerobically for 30 minute periods at least 4 times each week.

STRETCHING EXERCISES

Stretching exercises are also useful for stress management because we usually tense our muscles when we are stressed. By stretching, you reduce the muscle tension and as a result you begin to feel relaxed almost instantaneously.

Therefore, stretch every morning paying special attention to the muscles groups which get tense when you are stressed. These may be your neck, shoulder or back muscles.
During the day should you find that you are 'getting tense', take a moment to stretch and release the tension and you will have fewer aches at the end of the day.

WEIGHT BEARING EXERCISES

Strength training or weight bearing exercises are also helpful for managing stress as they demand total concentration. This is because when you are working on a particular muscle group, you focus your total concentration on that muscle and thus your attention is removed from your stressors.

As you train, do not strength train the same muscle groups for two consecutive days. Instead alternate them by working on the upper body muscles on one day and then on the lower body muscles the next day.

If you have been dormant and you would like to begin exercising regularly, first consult your doctor so that you can be cleared medically.

You can then begin by stretching for 5 minutes every morning and evening. Incorporate an aerobic activity that you enjoy into your daily schedule and gradually build it up to a total of 2 hours spread out over the week. Finally you can add on some weight bearing exercises under the supervision of a qualified person.

EAT HEALTHILY

When you are going through a stressful period especially one that is longstanding, your body needs all the nutritional support that it can get as it handles the various biochemical changes taking place.

Support your body by ensuring that you eat a well balanced diet every day. This diet should be rich in fish, fresh fruits, fresh vegetables and whole grain foods such as whole wheat bread and brown rice.

In addition, ensure all your meals contain protein rich foods such as fish, eggs, beans and yoghurt. These protein rich foods ensure slow and sustained release of glucose into the bloodstream and thus maintain steadier blood sugar levels.

Avoid meals composed mainly of sugary and processed foods as they result in a rapid rise and then a drop in the blood sugar level. This rapid drop may be accompanied by symptoms such as irritability and mood swings which you may already be experiencing as a result of your stressful situation and thus they will be worsened.

Eliminate or restrict your caffeine intake from all sources such as coffee, tea, chocolate, soft drinks as well as some pain and cold medications. Caffeine can worsen the nervousness, anxiety, palpitations and sleeplessness you may already be experiencing as a result of your stressful situation.

Increase your intake of antioxidant rich foods because when you are stressed, your body produces more free radicals. Perfect examples of antioxidant rich foods which mop up the free radicals include blueberries and many other berries, oranges and other citrus fruits.

Effect these changes in your diet in a way that will not further stress you by making small gradual changes that you can live with comfortably.

You can begin by adding one healthy food to your diet each week coupled with removing one unhealthy foodstuff until you have replaced all of the unwholesome foods you had been ingesting with healthy foods that you enjoy eating.

For example, you can ensure that you eat at least one brightly colored fruit or vegetable each day while halving your caffeine intake.

Once you have adjusted to this change, you can then ensure that you eat fish once a week as you get rid of one empty calorie processed food from your diet such as biscuits.

Then you can replace all your carbonated drinks with natural fruit juices.

Finally, ensure that you eat your meals in a peaceful and relaxed environment for **Better is a dry morsel with quietness, than a house full of feasting with strife.** (Proverbs 17:1)

GET ADEQUATE SLEEP

Since sleep is necessary for resting the mind and rejuvenating the body, see to it that you get 7 to 10 hours of sleep every night.

During the day, if possible, you can also indulge in an afternoon power nap of not more than 15 minutes and you will wake up refreshed.

If you find that you do not have enough hours to sleep at night, re-organize your schedule and pare down your activities. Cut out those that are not absolutely essential and those that contribute to increasing the stress in your already stressful life.

If you have difficulties falling asleep at night, establish a relaxation routine to let you disengage and unwind from your stressful day. This can include stretching for a few minutes, taking a warm bath, reading the Bible, saying a prayer and then listening to soothing music as you drift off to sleep. You should also set regular sleeping and waking times and abide by them.

If you have a tendency to ruminate over all your problems once you get into bed, meditate on the fact that **Unless the Lord builds the house, they labor in vain who build it; Unless the Lord guards the city, the watchman stays awake in vain. It is vain for you to rise up early, to sit up late, to eat the bread of sorrows; for so He gives His beloved sleep.** (Psalm 127: 1-2)

GET A MASSAGE

A massage is very effective relaxation technique.

This is due to the fact that emotional stress increases muscle tension and the manipulation that a muscle undergoes while it is being massaged helps reduces this tension in the muscle. And, once the tension is relieved, a person feels relaxed.

In addition to this there are numerous therapeutic benefits of massage such as pain relief which also play a role in stress management if the pain is contributing to the stress the person is experiencing.

Therefore, schedule regular professional massages and get the kinks ironed out of your body. A monthly massage for a person going through a lot of stress will improve their general well being.

Or, you can also ask a loved one such us a spouse to massage the tense areas of your body.

You can also experiment with self-massage and massage your scalp, temples, feet and other parts of your body that are within easy reach.

Enhance your massage experience by using massage oils containing relaxing oils such as lavender and chamomile.

MORE STRESS RELIEF ACTIVITIES

After you have incorporated the medical techniques in your lifestyle, you can also engage in other activities that help relieve stress and add pleasant moments to your days.

These pleasant moments punctuating your dreary days will contribute to making your weeks and months more tolerable and therefore you will be able to hold on for however long your waiting period may last.

Examples of simple stress relief activities that you can engage in include:
1. Remember the Sabbath
2. Sing praises to God
3. Engage in complementary hobbies
4. Establish your social support
5. Ease the suffering of the less fortunate

REMEMBER THE SABBATH

Remember the Sabbath day, to keep it holy. Six days you shall labor and do all your work, but the seventh day is the Sabbath of the Lord your God. In it you shall do no work. For in six days the Lord made the heavens and the earth, the sea, and all that is in them, and rested the seventh day. (Exodus 20: 8-11)

Heed God's command because stress is less likely to wear you down if you take regular breaks from your stressful life and you can do this by observing the Sabbath every week.

Therefore, keep your Sundays sacred, a day dedicated to God to spend more time communing with Him than you usually do on other days.

Slow down and reduce the noise in your environment. Avoid the customary activities of the workweek as this is not the day to run around trying to complete unfinished office work or housework.

Let Sunday be a special day when you take a break from mundane activities so that you can rest and be refreshed by the Lord.

To do so, engage in peaceful activities so that you can be calm within as you listen to what the He may be telling you. Go to church in the morning for many studies confirm that people of faith are healthier than nonbelievers and have speedier recovery from illnesses, surgery and addictions.

In the afternoon engage in rejuvenating activities such as watching your children play or swim, listening to soothing music, relaxing with friends, reading an inspiring book or you can just **Meditate within your heart on your bed, and be still.** (Psalm 4:4)

He tells us to **Be still, and know that I am God** (Psalm 46:10) so take the time to be still before the Lord and you will know that He is still in control of your situation no matter what your problems say.

If you must work on Sundays, then dedicate another day in the week when you are not working to the Lord so that you may rest and renew your spirit as you listen more deeply to Him.

SING PRAISES TO GOD

Singing songs of praise is a very effective method of making your waiting period more tolerable. Therefore, whenever you feel that your stressful situation is closing in on you or that your enemies and problems have cornered you and are breathing down your neck begin to praise God.

Begin to praise God as loudly as you can and from the bottom of your heart and you will scatter the forces of negativity and disperse the gloom that is threatening to engulf you.

You will also shake the foundations of the mental prisons that are trying to confine you, their doors will be flung open and your spirits will soar again. In addition, you will release pent up anguish and the chains of despondency will be broken as you dispel the despair.

So start to sing songs of praise when you feel yourself slipping and you will regain your footing. You will be able to stand firmly in your position because you will have been empowered, encouraged and emboldened by the power that is latent in praising God for He is **Enthroned in the praises**. (Psalm 22:3).

On some days it may not be easy to glorify God in the midst of your stressful situation because your heart may be broken and bleeding. On those days, do not desist from glorifying and worshipping Him.

Instead, praise Him and consider it sacrificial praise as you **continually offer the sacrifice of praise to God, that is, the fruit of our lips, giving thanks to His name.** (Hebrews 13:15)

Your praise can also be a praise of faith as we see in 2 Chronicles 20:21 where King Jehoshaphat **Appointed those who should sing to the Lord, and who should praise the beauty of holiness, as they went out before the army and were saying: Praise the Lord, for His mercy endures forever.**

They were going out in faith to take their positions against several large armies that were attacking them. They had not yet won the battle but they were already praising God because they had faith that they would emerge victorious because of His help. Their faith was so great that their choir marched in front of the army!

Their praise of faith was also so powerful that the Bible tells us that **When they begun to sing and to praise, the Lord set ambushes against the people of Ammon, Moab and Mount Seir, who had come against Judah; and they were defeated. For the people of Ammon and Moab stood up against the inhabitants of Mount Seir to utterly kill and destroy them. And when they had made an end of the inhabitants of Seir, they helped to destroy one another.** (2 Chronicles 20:22-23)

Therefore, praise God in the middle of your stressful situation as you stand firmly in your strategic position.

Praise Him for His goodness and faithfulness. **Praise Him for His mighty acts; Praise Him according to His excellent greatness!** (Psalm 150:2)

ENGAGE IN COMPLEMENTARY HOBBIES

You will be better able to bear your long waiting period if you have a pleasurable activity that you can regularly escape to engage in.

Identify an activity that complements your work, that you derive joy from and then do it regularly to take your mind away from your stressful situation.

For example, if your job is mentally challenging, escape to physically challenging activities that you enjoy such as exercising in a gym, playing squash, football, rugby or basketball.

If your work involves dealing with people especially addressing their complaints or fulfilling their demands, escape to solitary activities such as going to a spa for a facial, manicure or pedicure, knitting, painting, reading or gardening.

If you spend most of your time at work with computers and other machines, regularly escape to nature by going to the beach, hiking or taking your children to national parks. You can also engage in group activities such as singing in a choir.

After you have identified your enjoyable pastime, decide when you will engage in it so that you can look forward to it.

Engage in it regularly and use it to reward yourself for being strong in the face of all the challenges that you are facing and to encourage yourself to keep standing firmly as you wait patiently on the Lord.

EASE SUFFERING OF THE LESS FORTUNATE

Blessed is he who considers the poor; the Lord will deliver him in time of trouble. The Lord will preserve Him and keep him alive, and he will be blessed on the earth; You will not deliver him to the will of his enemies. The Lord will strengthen him on his bed of illness; You will sustain him on his sickbed. (Psalm 41:1-3)

Find time to help other people who are also in difficult situations. Your stressful situation may not have resolved, but you have sailed through the initial challenges and you can therefore advice and comfort someone who has just been shipwrecked.

Even if you are still be hurting on the inside, you can hold their hand, wipe their tears and listen with compassion. Tell them of how God's grace has held you, steadied you and enabled you to stand firmly in your position on your broken feet. Let them know that He too can heal them and strengthen them so that they too can rise up and walk again.

Take heed that you do not do your charitable deeds before men, to be seen by them. Otherwise, you have no reward from your Father in heaven. ☐ But when you do a charitable deed, do not let your left hand know what your right hand is doing; that your charitable deed may be in secret; and you Father who sees in secret will Himself reward you openly. (Matthew 6:1-4)

Feed the hungry, clothe the naked and visit prisoners. (Matthew 25: 34-36) Do it in a way that will result in them giving glory to God through Jesus Christ for providing them with assistance through you and not in a manner that will make them feel indebted to you.

By helping those who are less fortunate, you will also be helping yourself, for you will be able to take your mind off your problems and appreciate your blessings better.

Therefore, don't wait for your stressful situation to resolve before you can help others for you may miss many opportunities. Your testimony will also be more powerful when they see you standing firm and wiping their tears while your wounds are still bandaged.

ESTABLISH YOUR SOCIAL SUPPORT

Two are better than one, because they have a good reward for their labor. For if they fall, one will lift up his companion. (Ecclesiastes 4:9-10)

Establish a social support network and do not allow your work or your stressful situation to isolate you. Find people going through similar challenges or other stressful situations and spend time with them so that you can comfort and encourage each other, **Speaking to one another in psalms and hymns and spiritual songs.** (Ephesians 5: 19-20)

If you cannot find people in similar situations, then spend time with those who can support you. They may be your family or friends or church members. They can also be members of a social club with whom you have similar interests but ensure that they also have values similar to yours.

ALONE IN STRESSFUL SITUATION

In some stormy stressful situations, you may find yourself all alone trapped in your boat. You may find that the circumstances of your situation will not let you leave your boat to strengthen your social support system or allow you to engage in an enjoyable activity. Do not be disheartened for you can still enjoy your waiting period even if you are alone in prison or bound to your sick bed.

Observe the Sabbath in your own special way even if you are unable to attend a Church service. Offer praise to God at any time and even if you are not allowed to verbalize them for you can be sitting in silence yet **Singing and making melody in your heart to the Lord.** (Ephesians 5:19)

If you are unable to choose your diet, thank Him for whatever you are offered and He will bless it and it will bless your body. If you are unable to physically exercise, you can exercise your mind instead by reading the Bible and committing to memory as many Scriptures as you can. You can also read motivational books to stretch your mind.

If you don't have human companions, let Jesus be your entire support system. Strengthen your relationship with Him by regular prayer, Bible reading and by involving Him in each and every activity of your day until you fall asleep.

If you do this, you will find that even though your stressful situation may have limited you in certain aspects, you will grow in leaps and bounds spiritually as you spread your roots deeper and deeper into His Word and strengthen your walk with Him every day. He will fill all the voids in your life and you will find that you will still be able to enjoy your wait even if you are alone in your boat.

ACTION PLAN

1. Take at least 7 deep breaths every time you feel stressed.

2. Meditate for at least 10 minutes each day on Scriptures.

3. Visualize for at least 10 minutes each day.

4. Begin exercising for at least 30 minutes each week.

5. Go over your diet and see what changes you can effect to ensure you are eating healthily. Begin by adding one healthy food and removing one unhealthy food from your diet each week.

6. Schedule 7-10 hours of uninterrupted sleep each night.

7. Schedule a monthly professional massage.

8. Honor the Sabbath weekly by going to Church on Sunday.

9. Listen and sing along to Christian praise music every day. Consider joining a choir.

10. Engage in a pleasurable hobby at least once a week.

11. Establish your social support network by spending time with family and friends at least once a week.

12. Engage in at least one activity that will ease the suffering of a less fortunate member of your society.

LET US PRAY

I praise You with my whole heart;

I worship toward Your holy temple and praise Your name for Your loving-kindness.

I praise You for Your faithfulness.

I praise you for Your truth for You have magnified Your word above Your name.

Today I cry out to You, please answer me and make me bold with strength in my soul.

Thank you for though You are high above, you look kindly on us here below.

I live in the midst of stress, please revive me.

I walk and work in the midst of trouble, please save my life.

Stretch out Your hand against the wrath of my enemies and save me with Your right hand.

O Lord, please perfect that which concerns me.

Vindicate me and do not forsake me for Your love endures forever.
(Adapted from Psalm 138)

❧10☙

OBEY GOD
(Obedience)

Obey My voice, and I will be your God, and you shall be My people. And walk in all the ways that I have commanded you, that it may be well with you. (Jeremiah 7: 23)

Once you hear God's voice and He tells you what you to do, you must obey and do all that He commands so that it may be well with you.

He requires total obedience from you so if He tells you to let go of something, then you have to let go of it completely and forget about it. You have to obey the Lord in totality for partial obedience is tantamount to disobedience.

Learn from Saul who was given specific instructions by the Lord and told to "**Go and attack Amalek, and utterly destroy all that they have, and do not spare them. But kill both man and woman, infant and nursing child, ox and sheep, camel and donkey.**" (1 Samuel 15:3)

But Saul and the people spared Agag and the best of the sheep, the oxen, the fatlings, the lambs, and all that was good, and were unwilling to utterly destroy them. But everything despised and worthless, that they utterly destroyed. (1 Samuel 15:9)

Saul's excuse for his selective obedience was that the people had taken the best of the things so that they could sacrifice them to God. For this Saul was told that **To obey is better than sacrifice, and to heed than the fat of rams. For rebellion is as the sin of witchcraft, and stubbornness is as iniquity and idolatry.** (1 Samuel 15:22-23)

The Lord therefore does not like to be disobeyed and when you defy Him and do things your own way, you are no better than someone who is worshiping another god or practicing witchcraft. You are also no better than an idolater or a witchdoctor because both of you have turned your backs to God and decided to act contrary to His will.

Therefore, ensure that you obey all His instructions promptly because there is no way that you can justify your partial obedience or try to make it up to Him in another way.

TRUST AND OBEY

If the Lord asks you to walk in a certain direction, you have to walk in that direction and keep walking even if you do not know how you will get from point B to D because you cannot see C.

You are to keep walking in that direction even if you are wondering like Isaac in Genesis 22:7-8 when he asked his father, "Look, the fire, and the wood, but where is the lamb for a burnt offering? And Abraham said, My

son, God will provide for Himself the lamb for a burnt offering

Have the faith of Abraham and understand that you do not have to see everything just yet **For we walk by faith, not by sight.** (2 Corinthians 5:7)

You only have to set out in obedience in the direction that He has shown you one step at a time. Concentrate on getting from where you are to the next point B. Trust that when the time comes that you will need to see your point C, it will be provided and you will see it just as surely as Abraham saw the ram caught in the bush.

WALK BY FAITH

Learn to walk by faith even if the Lord is asking you to step out of the relative safety of your boat into the middle of the raging sea and walk on unstable waters.

He may be asking you to do something that may go against popular wisdom or that may seem humanly impossible to achieve, but you still have to obey and to step out in faith.

Do not reason within yourself and convince yourself that it is unwise to move from the relative security of your stressful job to the uncertain future of the full time ministry that He is calling you serve. Know that if God says, "Come", He is able to provide the means to support you as you walk through the raging waters if you will believe that He can do it.

Understand also that even when God has spoken to you and asked you to do something, you might still meet with challenges. The problems may not disappear just because you have stepped out in obedience.

Learn from Peter's experience when Jesus commanded him to get out of the boat and walk on the water. For **When Peter had come down out of the boat, he walked on the water to go to Jesus. But when he saw the wind was boisterous, he was afraid; and beginning to sink he cried out, saying, Lord, save me! And immediately Jesus stretched out His hand and caught him, and said to him, O you of little faith, why did you doubt?** (Matthew 14:29-31)

Peter was obedient and he stepped out in faith but the storm did not cease just because he had stepped on the water. Despite the turbulent wind, he was able to walk on the water without a problem until he moved his eyes from his Savior and begun to look at the raging sea. He noticed how boisterous the wind was and how rough the waves were and this made him afraid and he then begun to sink.

Therefore, as you walk in faith in the direction that the Lord has asked you to walk, do not focus your attention on the problems that may still be present in your stressful situation.

Do not also fear the persisting problems and problematic people or you will begin to drown.

Concentrate on doing what the Lord has asked you to do and you will find that you will make progress even though there are obstacles littering your path. Do not remove the focus of your attention from the Lord's ability to help you and sustain you through it all. Do not doubt for even one moment that He can help you achieve what He has asked you to do. Walk in faith and you will triumph over your stormy stressful situation.

OBEY WHEN YOU DO NOT UNDERSTAND

You have to obey God even if you do not understand why He is asking you to do certain things.

From the second book of Kings we learn about a widow whose creditor was coming to take possession of her two sons to be his slaves because she could not pay her debts. She then sought the man of God Elisha to find out from him what she was to do about her stressful situation.

He told her to **Go, borrow vessels from everywhere, from all your neighbors empty vessels; do not gather just a few.** (2 Kings 4:3) It may have seemed strange to her that the man of God wanted her to borrow even more yet she was already up to her neck in debt but the woman was obedient and did what the man of God had asked her to do.

She went and borrowed empty vessels and then she came home and begun to pour the oil that she had left in her house into them. When she had filled the last empty vessel that she had borrowed with oil, the oil ceased to flow.

From this we can see that the measure of her obedience was in direct proportion to the measure of blessings she received to help her resolve her stressful solution. If she had borrowed many empty vessels, in obediencc to the man of God, then she got a lot of oil to sell and therefore more money to pay her debts. But if she had borrowed just a few vessels, then she got just a little oil.

Similarly, you have to obey God even though you do not see how what He is telling you to do can solve the problems that you are facing in your stressful situation. Obey even when you do not understand and obey to the tiniest detail because He has a reason for everything that He tells us.

This woman's neighbors may not have understood why she was still borrowing and yet she could not pay the debts that she already had. They may have even advised her against borrowing anymore but she had to be obedient and do what the man of God had said.

This scenario may also apply to you, as you find that you do not have the support of the people around you as you set out to do what God has asked you to do. Know that you still have to obey God, with or without their support.

Don't waste your time and energy trying to explain yourself to people who don't see the logic in it. They might delay your progress or convince you with their worldly wisdom to disobey God. Focus only on what He has asked you to do and the distractions, temptations and ridicule will fall by the wayside.

Know that since you have been praying to God and waiting on God to provide you with a solution for your stressful situation, now that He has spoken, you have to continue looking up to Him and His Word for all the confirmation and encouragement that you may need.

Don't miss the awesome solution to your stressful situation that He has prepared for you because of public opinion. Single-mindedly set out to do what He has asked you to do and **Run in such a way that you may obtain it.** (1 Corinthians 9:24)

ACTION PLAN

1. Meditate on the following scripture:
To obey is better than sacrifice, and to heed than the fat of rams. For rebellion is as the sin of witchcraft, and stubbornness is as iniquity and idolatry. (1 Samuel 15:22)

2. Always remember:
- **S**   Seek the Lord
- **T**   Trust in the Lord
- **R**   Replace negative thoughts
- **E**   Eat healthily
- **S**   Stretch regularly
- **S**   Sleep adequately

LET US PRAY

Hear my just cause, O Lord and attend to my cry,
Give ear to my prayer which is not from deceitful lips.
Uphold my steps in Your paths, that my footsteps may not slip.

I have called upon you for You will hear me Lord
Show me Your marvelous loving-kindness by Your right hand, O You who save those who trust in You from those who rise up against them.
Keep me as the apple of Your eye;
Hide me under the shadow of Your wings,
From the wicked who oppress and stress me,
From the deadly enemies who surround me.

Arise, O Lord
Confront them and cast them down
Deliver my life from the wicked with Your sword and with Your hand.
(Adapted from Psalm 17)

After The Storm

Finally,
you will see your shore. It will be crystal clear where you have to go and what you have to do once you get there. You will also know that all will be provided as you set out obediently.

You will be a new creation.
You will walk on that beach as a new person. Your faith will have been fortified, your spiritual muscles strengthened and your inner self cleansed.

You will know God.
You will know God in a way you'd have never known Him if you hadn't lived through the storm and love Him in a way you'd have never loved Him if you hadn't seen Him snatch you from the jaws of death.

You will be useful.
He will have used the storm to shape you into a vessel that He can use for His divine purposes. You will be functional, dispensing the faith, hope and wisdom you reaped from your storm.

You will be at peace.
When you meet poisonous snakes, you will not fear for you know you can trample them underfoot. When you meet lions you will look them straight in the eye and continue walking on your path because you know Who is with you and what He has seen you through.

ABOUT THE AUTHOR

Dr. Miriam Kinai is a born again medical doctor who received her Bachelor of Medicine and Surgery degree from the University of Nairobi, her Diploma in Dermatology from Australia and her Clinical Training in Mind Body Medicine from Harvard Medical School. She is also a certified aromatherapist, trained Christian counselor and the author of many books.

RULES OF RELAXATION

Rules of Relaxation by Dr Miriam Kinai covers the A to Z of relaxation by teaching you 130 simple relaxation techniques to ensure that stress will never distress you.

Topics covered include: **A**ssert Yourself, **B**ask, **C**ount your Blessings, **D**rink Herbal Teas, **E**njoy Nature, **F**ormulate Realistic Goals, **G**et a Massage, **H**umor Yourself, **I**dentify Personal Stressors, **J**aunt, **K**eep pets, **L**isten to Music, **M**uffle Noise Stress, **N**ab a Nap, **O**ptimize Stress, **P**amper Yourself, **Q**uash Sin, **R**eason Rationally, **S**chedule News Fasts, **T**rust God, **U**se Cognitive Restructuring, **V**eto Worry, e**X**periment with Aromatherapy, **Y**ield to the Lord and **Z**ap Job Stress.

www.christianstressmanagement.com

SWORD WORDS

SWORD WORDS by Dr. Miriam Kinai teaches you how to fight the good fight (1 Timothy 6:12) using the SWORD of the Spirit which is the WORD of God (Ephesians 6:17).

It demystifies the enemy's strategies, explains the battle plan and elucidates tactical positioning and effective communication with your backup.

SWORD WORDS also contains compiled SWORD WORDS or Scriptures to help you fight for your family, finances, health, marriage, ministry, peace of mind, self confidence and sleep. It also contains SWORD WORDS to fight addiction, condemnation, confusion, danger, death, despair, fear, a foul mouth, impatience, laziness, loneliness, opposition, pride, sadness, vengeance, and worry.

www.christianstressmanagement.com

RESOLVING CONFLICTS JUST LIKE JESUS CHRIST

Resolving Conflicts just like Jesus Christ by Dr Miriam Kinai uses Biblical examples from Jesus Christ to King Solomon to teach you how to resolve conflicts effectively and increase the peace in your home, the productivity of your ministry and the profitability of your business.

Topics covered include Conflict Resolution Strategies (e.g. Pray Over It, Pay Attention, Proffer Something and Procure Something); Third Party Mediation Techniques (e.g. Set The Ground Rules, Select The Priorities, Suggest Possible Solutions and Step Through Impasses); Conflict Reduction and Prevention Strategies (e.g. Draw on Parables, Disagree Agreeably, Demarcate Your Boundaries and Depart From The Scoffer).

www.christianstressmanagement.com

MANAGING STRESS FOR TEENS

Managing Stress for Teens by Dr. Miriam Kinai teaches teenagers Biblical principles, medical techniques and life skills to manage common teenage stressors.

Topics covered include resisting alcohol, cigarettes, drugs and overcoming addiction.

It edifies them to resist peer pressure and fight sexual temptation, fornication, pornography and homosexuality.

It trains them to cope with family problems like abuse, problematic siblings and pressure from parents.

It teaches them manage worry, confusion, fear, despair, guilt, loneliness and shyness.

It schools them to deal with bullying, teachers and preparing for exams.

It clarifies Jesus and helps them answer "Who am I?" and "Why am I here?"

www.christianstressmanagement.com

MANAGING ACNE NATURALLY

Managing Acne Naturally by Dr. Miriam Kinai teaches you the natural remedies to treat acne. Topics covered include understanding your skin, "What is acne?", "What causes acne?", "What worsens acne?", the long-term effects of acne, back acne, preventing acne, understanding product labels and burying acne myths.

Natural acne therapies taught include aromatherapy, hydrotherapy, herbal therapy, juice therapy as well as good skin care habits to help reduce the frequency and severity of acne eruptions.. Dietary measures are also discussed as well as the role of nutritional supplements, physical exercise, stress management and other lifestyle modifications in the treatment of acne.

www.christianstressmanagement.com

NATURAL AND HOLISTIC DIABETES TREATMENT

Natural and Holistic Diabetes Treatment by Dr. Miriam Kinai teaches you how to manage diabetes naturally using a diabetic diet, stretching, aerobic and weigh bearing exercises, aromatherapy, relaxation techniques for stress management, loosing excess weight as well as aromatherapy using lavender and tea tree essential oils, herbs and dietary supplements.

It gives you practical example of these topics for instance by telling you the specific foods you should eat for your diabetic diet, walking you through the stress management plan, giving you aromatherapy recipes, telling you how to lose weight healthily and giving you the four steps to smoking cessation.

www.christianstressmanagement.com

HOW TO CREATE A CHRISTIAN SPA AT HOME

How to Create a Christian Spa at Home by Dr. Miriam Kinai teaches you how to create a sanctuary in your home where you can relax physically, mentally and recharge spiritually.

This book contains over thirty spa beauty and spa cuisine recipes that you can prepare at home. It teaches you how to prepare for a perfect home spa party.

It also tells you how to perform twenty five Christian Home Spa Activities. These include taking aromatherapy baths, having facials, manicures and pedicures, getting massages or massaging yourself, journaling, stretching exercises, enjoying healthy home spa cuisine and meditating on the Word of God.

www.christianstressmanagement.com

www.ingramcontent.com/pod-product-compliance
Lightning Source LLC
Chambersburg PA
CBHW060840050426
42453CB00008B/771